THE POLITICS
COMPANION

Matthew Stadlen and Harry Glass

Introduction by Andrew Marr

A THINK BOOK FOR

ROBSON BOOKS

The Cook's Companion
Edited by Jo Swinnerton
ISBN 1-86105-772-5

The Gardener's Companion
Edited by Vicky Bamforth
ISBN 1-86105-771-7

The Literary Companion
Edited by Emma Jones
ISBN 1-86105-798-9

The London Companion
Edited by Jo Swinnerton
ISBN 1-86105-799-7

The Moviegoer's Companion
Edited by Rhiannon Guy
ISBN 1-86105-797-0

The Traveller's Companion
Edited by Georgina Newbery and Rhiannon Guy
ISBN 1-86105-773-3

The Walker's Companion
Edited by Malcolm Tait
ISBN 1-86105-825-X

The Wildlife Companion
Edited by Malcolm Tait and Olive Tayler
ISBN 1-86105-770-9

SERIES EDITORS

Malcolm Tait, Emma Jones and Jo Swinnerton

Being Prime Minister is the easiest job in the world. Everyone else has an instrument to play. You just stand there and conduct.

James Callaghan

THINK

A Think Book
for Robson Books

First published in Great Britain in 2004 by
Robson Books
The Chrysalis Building, Bramley Road, London W10 6SP

An imprint of **Chrysalis** Books Group plc

Text © Think Publishing 2004
Design and layout © Think Publishing 2004
The moral rights of the authors have been asserted

Edited by Matthew Stadlen and Harry Glass
The Companion team: Vicky Bamforth, James Collins, Rhiannon Guy,
Emma Jones, Jo Swinnerton, Lou Millward Tait and Malcolm Tait

Think Publishing
The Pall Mall Deposit
124-128 Barlby Road, London W10 6BL
www.thinkpublishing.co.uk

ISBN 1-86105-796-2

Printed and bound by Clays Ltd, Bungay, Suffolk NR35 1ED

*A man may die, nations may rise and fall,
but an idea lives on.*

JFK

A VOTE OF THANKS

This book would not have been possible without the
research, ideas, and dogged support of:

Dominic Bates, Paul Bates, Adam Biles,
Jules and Ollie Campbell, Gwenny Campbell, Professor Paul
Cartledge, Richard Dowden, Ed Dowding, Ken Eaton,
Stuart Fance, Abbe Fawcett, Kim Gifford, Alan Gill,
Lucy Grewcock, Ivo Grigorov, Lisa Holm, Nikki Illes,
Boris Johnson MP, Anatole Kaletsky, Charles Kennedy MP,
Neil Kinnock, Monica Kroll, Rachel Kurzfield,
Michael Mansfield QC, Chris Moncrieff, Bryn Morgan,
Charli Morgan, Mark Oaten MP, Professor Tim Peto,
Peter Riddell, Hugh Roberts, Alan Rusbridger, Xan Smiley,
Jonathan Stadlen, Heidi Stadlen, Nathalie Stahelin, Stanley,
Chris Sturdy, Jennifer Style and Martin Wolf

INTRODUCTION

There are very many books about politics: wearisomely many. There are biographies the size of small cottages; awesomely grand memoirs by the entirely unmemorable; squat, gold-embossed official looking lists of MPs, political facts, election statistics and peers. There are books of political theory, many of them mad. There are academic tomes, barely in English, and there are those fine collector's items, biographies of obscure dictators published by the late Robert Maxwell. There are, in short, very nearly enough books about politics. My house has very little space left to live in.

Where this companion differs from most of the above is that it is slim, amusing and almost entirely useless. It is not a gazetteer or a work of reference – or if it is, there must be some strange work you're engaged in. It contains slivers and fragments, crumbs and surprises. It should catch the eye, and keep you reading for a couple of pages. It should be put down and picked up, again and again. It may well persuade you to dig deeper – to risk back pain with one of those grossly overweight American presidential autobiographies for instance, or turn to Trollope. I learned many things from it and all of them pleasingly useless. It will rest with others of my 'pick-ups', gradually becoming dog-eared, in one of the smaller rooms of the house, at knee height.

Andrew Marr
Political Editor, BBC

ASSASSINATION ATTEMPTS

On 15 February 1933, Giuseppe Zangara, an immigrant, fired five shots at the President-elect Franklin D Roosevelt. Roosevelt was delivering a speech from his open car in Miami, Florida. Zangara missed Roosevelt but hit the Chicago mayor Anton Cermak. The mayor later died of his wounds. Zangara had suffered from severe stomach pains and was disaffected with life during the Depression. Only about five feet tall, he had to stand on a chair to direct his shot at the President-elect, and one report suggested that he missed his target because the chair wobbled. On 20 March 1933, just two weeks after Cermak died and a little over a month after the shooting, Zangara was electrocuted. Zangara's last words before his execution were reportedly 'Adios to the world!'

THE POWER AGE

- Fidel Castro became Cuba's Head of State at the age of 32.
- Colonel Muammar Gaddafi became de facto Chief of State in Libya at the age of 27.
- Jean-Claude 'Baby Doc' Duvalier, became President for Life of Haiti at the age of 19. He may also have been the youngest ex-President for Life – he was finished by the age of 34, when he fled to France.
- Deng Xiaoping became the de facto ruler of China at the age of 72.
- Senator Strom Thurmond became chairman of United States Armed Services Committee when he was 92.
- Dr Hastings Kamuzu Banda never revealed his age, but remained Life President of Malawi well into his 90s. It is thought he was born in 1898, and so would have been 96 when he was beaten at election in 1994.

RULES OF THE HOUSE

The practice of the Commons Prayer is believed to have started in about 1558, and was an established ritual by 1567. The present form of prayers is thought to date from the Restoration. Every session in the House kicks off with prayers, and members of the public may not be present at this time. Members have to stand facing the wall behind them, which means the two main parties stand facing away from each other. It is traditional for members not to kneel. This dates from a time when they would have found it difficult to do so wearing their swords.

The Speaker's Chaplain reads the prayers in the Commons, although on rare occasions (and in the absence of any clergy) the Speaker reads them instead.

Number of seconds Margaret Thatcher claims it takes her to make up her mind up about a man

Blair had only been in Number Ten once before, for an official dinner with President Clinton in November 1996. 'I remember walking down the corridor of Downing Street for only the very second time in my life,' he said later. 'In a little room just off the Cabinet room,' he met Sir Robin Butler, the Cabinet Secretary, who greeted him with the words, 'Well, you're in charge. What are we going to do, then?'

In a risky off-text preamble to his 1998 party conference speech, Blair said: 'When you become Prime Minister the first thing they do – after telling you how to launch the nuclear bomb – is to take your passport from you, and then the rest of the time trying to get you to travel around the world.' After finding out how to authorise the use of the Trident missiles against which he and many Labour members had once campaigned, he was introduced and shown around. John Major had left a bottle of champagne with a note for him and Cherie saying, 'It's a great job – enjoy it.'

John Rentoul, *Tony Blair Prime Minister*

VERSE AND WORSE

Mary Mary quite contrary,
How does your garden grow?
With silver bells and cockle shells
And pretty maids all in a row.

In this apparently innocent nursery rhyme, 'Mary' refers to Mary Tudor, or 'Bloody Mary', the daughter of King Henry VIII. The Queen was a hardened Catholic who had many of her Protestant enemies tortured and executed. The garden is thought to represent the graveyards of Protestants. The silver bells and cockle shells are euphemisms for instruments of torture such as thumbscrews and iron masks and the 'maids' refer to a guillotine-like structure that was used for executions.

FIFTY PER CENT WOOL, FIFTY PER CENT LORD

The Queen sits on the 'throne' in the Lords, the Speaker of the Commons has the 'chair', and the Lord Chancellor, Speaker of the House of Lords, sits on the 'woolsack' – a large seat stuffed with wool. Introduced by King Edward III in the fourteenth century as a reminder that England's traditional source of wealth was the wool trade, the Lord Chancellor had his bottom cushioned by English wool alone. It has occasionally been re-stuffed to keep it firm, and the Chancellor now has the pleasure of sitting on a collection of wools from various Commonwealth nations, to symbolise unity.

During the Rio de Janeiro mayoral elections in 1988, the anti-establishment Brazilian Banana Party was fronted by Tiao, a chimpanzee, whose slogan was: 'Vote monkey – get monkey'. Tiao came third out of 12 candidates, winning over 400,000 votes. In defeat, he made a return to Rio's zoo, presumably to plan his next assault on city politics. His comeback never materialised however, and he died in December 1996 aged 33. The Brazilians of Sao Paulo had already tried installing the zoo's rhinoceros as mayor of the city. On 4 October 1958 Cacareco the rhino actually won the state election with an estimated 100,000 votes. But the people's choice was ignored and the second-placed candidate took office.

When President Vladimir Putin endorsed the candidacy of Valentina Matviyenko for governor of St Petersburg in 2003, supporters of her rival, Anna Markova, proposed a horse as candidate. Putin's endorsement was against election rules, and the horse was their way of protesting. One of the other contenders, Sergei Pryanishnikov, a pornographic movie producer who had promised to make the city the 'erotic capital of Europe', had already fallen by the wayside. But the horse knew it stood a chance with its four legs to Matviyenko's two, and fought on. Political commentators welcomed 'the horse vote',

and one magazine editor said: 'I would vote for the horse because it doesn't lie and doesn't use dirty tactics.' However, as the horse couldn't talk, write or host large dinner parties, common sense finally prevailed and its late surge collapsed.

Roman emperor Gaius Caesar Augustus Germanicus was more commonly known as Caligula because when he was a youngster he ran around in a mini pair of military sandals – 'caligae'. When he became emperor he suffered an illness that nearly killed him, and his contemporaries blamed this for his increasingly eccentric and depraved behaviour. He housed his favourite horse Incitatus in a carved-ivory stable box and would invite guests for dinner in the horse's name. The animal was even asked to join them on occasion. Caligula is thought to have detested the senators so much that he decided to appoint Incitatus as one.

A dog called Suening ruled Norway for three years in the eleventh century, giving a whole new meaning to the term 'political animal'. Suening routinely signed paw-print decrees and the dog's reign was only brought to an end when he tried to break up a fight between a wolf and a sheep. Unfortunately for Suening, the wolf tore open his throat with his fangs.

Downing Street was once just a boggy island situated between two branches of the River Tyburn, which flowed from Hampstead Heath to the Thames. The Romans selected the site for settlement because of its location near a ford on the Thames, which joined the road to Kent. In the tenth century, King Canute built a royal palace there and archaeological clues even suggest that the area was used as a brewery, owned by the Abbey of Abingdon.

By the 1500s, the site had sobered up and the first house was built there. Queen Elizabeth I leased it rent-free for life to Thomas Knyvet, MP for Thetford and the man who arrested Guy Fawkes for his part in the Gunpowder Plot in 1605. After Knyvet and his wife died, Knyvet House was renamed Hampden House and passed to the Knyvets' niece whose nephew was Oliver Cromwell.

Harvard graduate George Downing built the most familiar parts of the house – the fronts of Number 10 and Number 11. Downing bought the site during the brief period of Parliamentary rule after the death of Charles I. He supported Cromwell but worked for Charles II once the monarchy was restored and betrayed some of his former colleagues. His portrait now hangs in the entrance hall of Number 10.

First Lord of the Treasury Sir Robert Walpole took up residence in 1735 when the last tenant, a Mr Chicken, moved out. In the spirit of looking after your own, Walpole secured the house for all future First Lords of the Treasury. The letterbox on the front door is therefore inscribed with this title, rather than that of Prime Minister, although every PM is also the first Lord of the Treasury. Despite having his name on the door, Tony Blair, in order to accommodate his family, swapped houses with Number 11 resident Gordon Brown, the Chancellor of the Exchequer, in 1997.

INSIDE CENTRAL GOVERNMENT

While most of us know we can vote a government into power, not many of us know that we can complain about them once they're there. If you have suffered injustice due to poor administration by a government department, you can complain to the Parliamentary Ombudsman. If the Ombudsman agrees that you have good grounds for complaint, he can recommend that the guilty organisation provide a remedy. However, sadly, the Ombudsman has only limited powers, and he or she cannot then enforce his findings, which can leave you back in the hands of the department you complained about in the first place.

The British are involved in a number of territorial disputes around the world. For example…

In 2002, the residents of **Gibraltar** voted overwhelmingly in a referendum against a 'total shared sovereignty' arrangement worked out between Spain and the UK. The British captured Gibraltar from the Spanish early in the eighteenth century. The island off the coast of southern Spain was formally ceded to the Empire.

Mauritius claims the Chagos Archipelago, a British territory in the Indian Ocean. Mauritius Prime Minister Paul Berenger wrote to Tony Blair in 2004, after legal advice from international lawyers suggested the secession of the islands from Mauritius by the British in 1965 was illegal. The British Government forced around 2,000 residents to leave the Chagos islands between 1967 and 1973, so the US could build a military airbase on the island of Diego Garcia, the biggest of the archipelago. A court ruling in November 2000 quashed the 1971 Immigration Ordinance, which was enacted at the time of the removals to give them legal authority, and also granted the islanders British citizenship.

The **Falklands**, a group of 200 small islands between Argentina and the Arctic Circle, became a British territory in 1833. The Argentines had briefly settled the islands in 1820 after they gained independence from Spain in 1916. Argentine forces occupied the Falkland Islands in April 1982. The Argentines had long claimed sovereignty over the islands they called Islas Malvinas. The UK sent a force to re-capture the islands and won the war in June, in which around 700 Argentines were killed. Argentina continues to dispute the sovereignty of the islands which still appear on national maps as Argentine territory. Argentina also lays claim to South Georgia, the first landing place for Argentine forces during the Falklands War, and to the Sandwich Islands. The UK withdrew its tiny contingent of troops from South Georgia to the Falklands in 2001.

John can't decide what to vote at the next election, so he puts three blue balls, three red balls and three yellow balls into a bag, and draws them out one by one, whichever colour being the last earning his vote. The first three balls he draws out are two red and one blue. What is now the likelihood that he will vote for the yellow party?
Answer on page 153.

Number of times Michael Howard evaded Jeremy Paxman's question on 'Newsnight' on whether he threatened to overrule prisons chief Derek Lewis

NO POINT IN RUSSIAN THE GAME

The White Palace might never have been captured during the Russian Revolution if the Cossacks hadn't insisted on completing their inter-regiment croquet tournament.

QUOTE UNQUOTE

If they will stop telling lies about the Democrats, we will stop telling the truth about them.
Adlai Stevenson, Democrat Presidential Candidate, 1900–1965

DISORDER IN THE HOUSE

In July 1893 a fight erupted at the end of the Committee Stage of the Home Rule Bill when the Irish Nationalist MP Thomas Power O'Connor called Joseph Chamberlain a 'Judas'. Punches were thrown, members grappled and no doubt a few hats were squashed. Chamberlain's biographer JL Garvin described the scene: 'One could see the teeth set, the eyes flashing, faces aflame with wrath and a thicket of closed fists beating about in wild confusion.' The Sergeant at Arms, having lost control of the Chamber in the mêlée, attempted to restore some order elsewhere. He was seen telling a member who was watching the brawl from a safe distance: 'I beg your pardon, but you're standing up with your hat on, which you know is a breach of order.'

Neil Hamilton had been mired in allegations of sleaze for three years by the time, in May 1997, John Major finally called a General Election. Conservative headquarters had begged Hamilton not to stand for re-election, but in a gesture of overweening arrogance, he refused to go quietly. At that point, the Labour and Liberal Democrat candidates agreed to stand aside to allow the former war-reporter Martin Bell to run against Hamilton as an independent 'anti-sleaze' campaigner. The battle between the two immediately became one of the highlights of the election, drawing in reporters and camera crews from as far away as Australia and Japan. One of these reporters tipped off the Hamiltons that Martin Bell was due to hold a news conference later that morning on Knutsford Heath, a former racecourse. As Christine Hamilton recalls it, 'Neil said "Is he indeed! Well, I've got some questions to ask him."' The sitting MP went upstairs to change into a suit referred to ever afterwards as being in 'bounder check' or as 'the Terry Thomas outfit'. ('It's so unfair,' she says. 'It was a perfectly normal Prince of Wales check.') Yet it was not her husband who was to be the main attraction, but the extraordinary apparition at his side. Confronting the independent candidate, she boomed at him, 'Do you accept my husband is innocent?' again and again. Bell was embarrassed, confused and lost for words. Hers was the sort of performance which, one columnist commented later, displayed the valour of an early Christian martyr, making you wonder how Britain ever lost its empire. But it was, in the end, to no avail. Neil Hamilton's defeat by Martin Bell was as comprehensive a humiliation as any politician has suffered in modern politics: it takes some astonishing public distaste to turn a Conservative majority of 22,000 votes into defeat by a margin of 11,000. Bell made a slightly prim speech at the count, while Hamilton simply said that he was 'devastated'.

Jeremy Paxman,
The Political Animal

MARRIED ON THE JOB

John Tyler was the first President of the United States to get married while in office. He and his fiancée Julia Gardiner made their vows on 26 June 1844 when Tyler was 54 and his wife 24, the greatest age difference in a US presidential marriage. The couple went on to have seven children. Tyler already had eight children from his marriage to his first wife, Letitia, who died in the White House of a stroke in 1842. Since then both Grover Cleveland and Woodrow Wilson have been married while in office.

SHAKESPEARE ON POLITICS

A week is a long time in politics. So, for some people, is a day.

MARK ANTONY:
But yesterday the word of Caesar might
Have stood against the world; now lies he there,
And none so poor to do him reverence.

Julius Caesar, Act III Scene ii

COOKE'S TRAVELS

Journalist and broadcaster Alistair Cooke once earned the unusual distinction of being invited to address the Congress of the United States. Cooke enjoyed the honour on its 200th anniversary in 1974, although during his address he was, for once, almost lost for words. He did manage to get out a joke, which was: 'I gratefully accept your nomination for President of the United States.' Cooke was most famous in his native Britain for his weekly radio broadcast, *Letter from America*, in which he commented on the week's news from a US perspective. The programme lasted 58 years and was the longest running series ever presented by one person, a record made possible by the fact that Cooke was still broadcasting until a few weeks before his death at the age of 95 on 30 March 2004.

Cooke's address to Congress placed him in very exalted company; Winston Churchill, Clement Attlee, Margaret Thatcher, Tony Blair and Queen Elizabeth II have also been invited to address Congress.

WHJ (WHITE HOUSE JARGON)

POTUS	President of the United States
FLOTUS	First Lady of the United States
CSG	Counter-terrorism Security Group
PEOC	Presidential Emergency Operations Center
Norad	North American Aerospace Defence Command
CAP	Combat Air Patrol
COG	Continuity of Government
FAA	Federal Aviation Administration
DoD	Department of Defense
SIOC	Strategic Information and Operations Center (FBI command center)

ASSASSINATION ATTEMPTS

On 19 March 2004, the day before national elections, the Taiwanese President Chen Shui-Bian was shot at from within cheering crowds as he drove through his home town of Tainan with the Vice President Annette Lu in an open-top red jeep. The shots were drowned out by firecrackers in the crowd. The President and Vice President were rushed to Chimei Hospital. Chen needed 11 stitches in a four-inch flesh wound across his abdomen and a used bullet was found in his jacket pocket. Lu suffered a minor knee wound.

Chen was re-elected the following day, beating his opponent Lien Chan by a tiny margin. Sympathy votes were thought to have proved decisive. The opposition leader Huang Chao-shun complained to the TVBS television network that 'The shooting may have cost us a million votes.' Conspiracy theories ruled. Lien's supporters went so far as to suggest that the shooting could have been staged for political purposes. There were also claims that bookmakers wanted the President dead to pre-empt substantial losses if he won the election.

The attempt on Chen's life is thought not to have been the first. His wife was paralysed from the waist down in 1985 after a truck ran her over. Many believe that Chen was the intended victim. But Chen did not lose his charismatic turn of phrase. When Lien Chan called him 'unreliable' in Taiwan's first-ever televised presidential debate, Chen replied, 'My hairstyle has never changed over the years, nor my love for my wife.'

QUOTE UNQUOTE

I am extraordinarily patient, provided I get my own way in the end.
Margaret Thatcher, Prime Minister 1979–1990

LOSING THE RACE

Presidential candidates who were pipped to the post

2000	Al Gore, *Democrat*
1996	Robert Dole, *Republican*
1992	George Bush (Snr), *Republican*
1988	Michael Dukakis, *Democrat*
1984	Walter Mondale, *Democrat*
1980	Jimmy Carter, *Democrat*
1976	Gerald Ford, *Republican*
1972	George McGovern, *Democrat*
1968	Hubert Humphrey, *Democrat*
1964	Barry Goldwater, *Republican*
1960	Richard Nixon, *Republican*

THAT'S NO LADY, THAT'S MY WIFE

When actress Jamie Lee Curtis got married, she might not have expected her wifely duties to include turning up at the House of Lords in 1998 for the state opening of parliament. The movie star and daughter of Hollywood legends Tony Curtis and Janet Leigh is married to the writer and director Christopher Guest, who became the fifth Baron Haden-Guest of Saling, Essex, when his father, Lord Peter Haden-Guest, died of cancer. Curtis may be used to the red-carpet treatment, but she hasn't let her new role go to her head, as she later explained in an interview with *Hello!* magazine: 'Nobody addresses me as Lady Guest anywhere except perhaps at the House of Lords. It's what they do there'. Among other things, we hope.

THE UNELECTABLES

Some of the people who cannot stand for Parliament in the UK

- Peers who sit in the House of Lords
- Bishops who are entitled to sit and vote in the House of Lords
- People who hold public offices, such as judges, civil servants, members of the armed forces, police
- People under 21 years of age
- People who are not subjects of Britain, the Commonwealth or the Republic of Ireland
- People with severe mental disorders
- People jailed for more than 12 months
- Undischarged bankrupts

POLITICS IN WRITING

He was Prime Minister at last at the age of sixty-five, apart from his immediate predecessor the oldest person since Campbell-Bannerman to come to that office for the first time. It was also almost forty years after he had first been elected to Parliament. He took over in the most perilous circumstances in which any Prime Minister has ever come to office. And there were political as well as military perils. He was not the choice of the King. He was not the choice of the Whitehall estab-lishment, which reacted with varying degrees of dismay to the prospect of his alleged wildness. And he was not the choice of the majority party in the House of Commons. In an inchoate way, how-ever, he was, or quickly became, the accepted champion of the nation in the eyes of both public and press. And those who had initially been reluctant and suspicious, from Sovereign to permanent secretaries, fairly quickly came round to his indispensability.

Roy Jenkins, *Churchill*

1764 Boston merchants begin a boycott of British luxury goods.

1765 The Stamp Act is passed in March by the British parliament. The first direct tax is imposed on the US colonies and is levied on all printed materials to cover the costs of supporting 10,000 regular soldiers in North America. The colonists unite in protest. 'No taxation without representation' goes the chant and there is rioting.

1766 The Stamp Act is repealed in March, but the Declaratory Act is passed the same day and the British government is empowered to tax the colonies.

1767 The Townshend Revenue Acts are passed in June. The Townshend Duties, named after Charles Townshend, Chancellor of the Exchequer, impose taxes on imports to the colonies such as paper, tea, glass, lead and paints. The colonists protest and threaten embargoes on British goods.

1770 The Boston Massacre. Colonists attack a British sentry in Massachusetts and five colonists are killed. Lord North becomes Prime Minister. All the Townshend Duties apart from the one levied on tea is repealed.

1773 The Boston Tea Party. The East India Company claims that the colonists buy their tea from smugglers to evade import taxes. North authorises direct shipments to the US in an attempt to undercut the smugglers' prices, but colonial dockworkers refuse to unload the tea. On 16 December a party of men dressed as Mohawk Indians and calling themselves the 'Sons of Liberty' board three British ships, the Beaver, the Eleanor and the Dartmouth docked in Griffin's Wharf, Boston. The rebels throw 45 tonnes of tea into the harbour.

1775 Skirmishes at Lexington. A colonial army is raised with George Washington in command.

1776 The British fleet arrive in St Lawrence. The American Declaration of Independence is signed on 4 July.

1778 The French sign an alliance with the US.

1779 Spain enters the war on the American side.

1780 Holland begins hostilities, protesting at British seizures of contraband from neutral ships.

1781 The British General Cornwallis surrenders to Washington at Yorktown.

1782 North resigns as Prime Minister and the Preliminary Peace Treaty is signed in Paris.

1783 The British recognise the independence of the Thirteen States as the United States of America.

1784 The Treaty of Paris is ratified by Congress on 14 January and the Revolutionary War officially ends.

1788 The President of Congress formally announces on 2 July that the Constitution of the US has come into effect.

Slack benchers

SHAKESPEARE ON POLITICS

Politicians have to watch their backs. Political coups can be fatal, as Caesar found out the hard way

> CAESAR:
> Let me have men about me that are fat;
> Sleek-headed men, and such as sleep o'nights.
> Yond Cassius has a lean and hungry look;
> He thinks too much. Such men are dangerous.

> ***Julius Caesar*, Act I Scene ii**

TRAVELLING TUCK SHOP

In the build-up to the 2001 General Election, the Liberal Democrats stocked up with 4,600 cans of Diet Coke, 1,700 bananas, 244 packets of Jaffa Cakes and 200 gallons of mineral water to sustain their campaign bus. They still came third.

WHO CAN BE PRESIDENT?

Section 1 of Article 2 of the US Constitution stipulates that to become President you must be a natural-born citizen of the US, you must be at least 35 years old and you have to have lived in the US for at least 14 years. It is widely accepted that this applies to citizens born outside the States whose parents are US citizens. People born in Guam, Puerto Rico and the US Virgin Islands are legally defined as natural-born citizens.

You also can't have been President before, at least not more than twice. President Franklin D Roosevelt spent 12 years in office from 1933–1945, the longest term of any President. But the 22nd Amendment, introduced in 1951, states that Presidents cannot serve more than two four-year terms. This applies even if they have served for only two or more years of one of those terms.

The rules are more relaxed for membership of the Senate. According to Article 1 Section 3, candidates for the Senate must be at least 30 years of age, must have lived in the US for nine years, and must be a resident of the state when elected.

According to Article 1 Section 2, candidates for the House of Representatives must be at least 25 years of age, must have lived in the US for seven years, and must be a resident of the state when elected.

QUOTE UNQUOTE

The nine most terrifying words in the English language are, 'I'm from the government and I'm here to help.'
Ronald Reagan, US President 1981–1989

WORLD'S LONGEST-REIGNING MONARCHS

Name	Dates	Length of Rule	Age of Accession
1. King Louis XIV	1643–1715	72 years	5
2. King John II	1858–1929	71 years	18
3. Emperor Franz-Josef	1848–1916	67 years	18
4. Queen Victoria	1837–1901	63 years	18
5. Emperor Hirohito	1926–1989	62 years	25
6. Emperor K'ang His	1661–1722	61 years	8
7. King Sobhuza II	1921–1982	60 years	22
8. Emperor Ch'ien Lung	1735–1796	60 years	25
9. King Christian IV	1588–1648	59 years	11
10. King George III	1760–1820	59 years	22

Abraham Lincoln was elected to Congress in 1846.
John F Kennedy was elected to Congress in 1946.

Abraham Lincoln was elected President in 1860.
John F Kennedy was elected President in 1960.

The names Lincoln and Kennedy each contain seven letters.
Both were particularly concerned with civil rights.
Both wives lost children while living in the White House.

Both Presidents were shot on a Friday.
Both were shot in the head.

Kennedy's secretary was named Lincoln.
Lincoln's secretary was named Kennedy.

Both were assassinated by Southerners.
Both were succeeded by Southerners.

John Wilkes Booth, who shot Lincoln, was born in 1839.
Lee Harvey Oswald, who was accused of shooting Kennedy, was born in 1939.

Booth ran from the theatre and was caught in a storage barn.
Oswald ran from a warehouse and was caught in a movie theatre.

Booth and Oswald were both killed before their trials.

LA CICCIOLINA

When Ilona Staller ran for election in Italy in 1987, she campaigned under her porn star stage name, Cicciolina. The Radical Party candidate won a seat in parliament and continued to act in hardcore movies for the next two years. In September 1990, during the build-up to the Gulf War, Cicciolina did her bit for peace by offering to sleep with the Iraqi leader. 'I am available to make love with Saddam Hussein to achieve peace in the Middle East,' she announced. She renewed the offer in October 2002. The ex-porn star is famous for undressing off set as well as on. In Italy she revealed her left breast to emphasise her left-wing politics. She once said, 'My breasts have never done anyone any harm, while bin Laden's war has caused thousands of victims.' But Hungarian-born Cicciolina's political luck ran out when she failed to be chosen to stand for election in Hungary. She subsequently claimed that one of the other parties had run a dirty tricks campaign to keep her out, and protested that this was 'not fair and not healthy'.

'I'VE GOT THESE TICKETS...'

The following 15 people turned down Abraham Lincoln's theatre invitation on the night he was assassinated:

Name	Reason
Mr and Mrs Ulysses S Grant	*Visiting children*
Mr and Mrs Edwin Stanton	*Declined*
Thomas Eckert	*Work commitments*
Schuyler Colfax	*Holiday plans*
George Ashmun	*Previous engagement*
Richard J Oglesby	*Visiting friends*
Richard Yates	*Previous engagement*
General Isham N Haynie	*Previous engagement*
William A Howard	*Planned to leave Washington*
Mr and Mrs William H Wallace	*Weariness*
Noah Brooks	*Illness*
Robert Lincoln (eldest son)	*Early night*

Henry Rathbone and Clara Harris accepted the invitation

PUZZLING POLITICS

My first is in right but never in left
My second's in Europe which I think is the best
My third is in sailing and also in sea
My fourth is in Wedgie Benn's favourite drink – tea
My fifth is in history but not in remorse
My whole's a PM who sounds covered with gorse
Answer on page 153.

O COME ALL YE TOURISTS

The Palace of Westminster opened to the public in the summer of 2000 for a trial period. Unfortunately, the experiment was not a great success. The final visitor numbers of 40,580 did not match the expected minimum of 55,980. Also, a report into the scheme found that a typical visitor to the Houses of Parliament was a middle-class white Londoner. Guests proved keener on buying postcards than on the Pugin-style silk ties. Merchandise sales of £138,551 reached nowhere near the target of £478,400 and the merchandising project made a loss of £15,000. It was reported that the guides were to be told to spend more time waxing lyrical over Pugin's contribution to Parliamentary artwork in the hope that the Pugin-themed products would become more popular. The Palace of Westminster remains open to tourists during the summer recess.

The article in Declaration of Human Rights stating everyone has the right to rest and leisure, limiting working hours

HE SAID IT FIRST

Ask not what your country can do for you – this phrase was famously used by John F Kennedy, but it was President Warren Harding who gave him the idea. Harding said 'we must have a citizenship less concerned about what the government can do for it and more anxious about what it can do for the nation'.

THE FIRST COUNTRIES TO GIVE WOMEN THE VOTE

New Zealand (1893)
Australia (1902)
Finland (1906)
Norway (1913)
Denmark and Iceland (a Danish dependency until 1918) (1915)
USSR (1917)
Austria (1918)
Canada, excluding Quebec (1918)
Germany (1918)
Great Britain and Ireland (1918)
Estonia, Latvia and Poland (1918)
Netherlands (1919)

All were preceded by the Isle of Man, which gave women the vote in 1880, and by the US state of Wyoming, which did the same in 1869.

POLITICS IN WRITING

The House of Commons is like a church. The vaulted roofs and stained glass windows, the rows of statues of great statesmen of the past, the echoing halls, the soft-footed attendants and the whispered conversations, contrast depressingly with the crowded meetings and the clang and clash of hot opinions he has just left behind in the election campaign. Here he is, a tribune of the people, coming to make his voice heard in the seats of power. Instead, it seems he is expected to worship; and the most conservative of all religions – ancestor worship.
Aneurin Bevan, *In Place of Fear*

BUT WHAT DOES IT MEAN?

The world politics comes from *polis* (city) and *polites* (citizen). At first it was to do with citizens' rights, but over the centuries it has come to mean the theory and practice of government. Candidate comes from the Roman *candidatus*, which means 'clothed in white', as someone would have been if they were seeking office.

When the police were ordered to find a less confrontational way of dealing with the drunk and disorderly, they took to their new role with great enthusiasm

THAT'S TENACIOUS

The longest-serving Presidents in power in 2004

Name	Took power in
Fidel Castro, Cuba	*1 January 1959*
General Gnassingbé Eyadéma, Togo	*14 April 1967*
El Hadj Omar Bongo, Gabon	*2 December 1967*
Colonel Muammar Gaddafi, Libya	*1 September 1969*
Zayid bin Sultan al-Nuhayyan, UAE	*2 December 1971*
Ali Abdullah Saleh, Yemen	*17 July 1978*
Maumoon Abdul Gayoom, Maldives	*11 November 1978*
Teodoro Obiang Nguema Mbasogo, Equatorial Guinea	*3 August 1979*
José Eduardo dos Santos, Angola	*21 September 1979*

VOTING POWER

The ministers of the EU member states meet within the Council of the European Union. Each country is represented by the minister responsible for the issue on the agenda. Decisions are taken by vote. The bigger the country's population, the more votes it has. The process is not strictly proportional and is adjusted in favour of the less populous countries, but it does put certain countries in a position of strength.

Germany	29
United Kingdom	29
France	29
Italy	29
Spain	27
Poland	27
Netherlands	13
Greece	12
Czech Republic	12
Belgium	12
Hungary	12
Portugal	12
Sweden	10
Austria	10
Slovakia	7
Denmark	7
Finland	7
Ireland	7
Lithuania	7
Latvia	4
Slovenia	4
Estonia	4
Cyprus	4
Luxembourg	4
Malta	3
Total	321

POLITICS IN WRITING

The county of Yorkshire, which contains near a million souls, sends two county members; and so does the county of Rutland which contains not a hundredth part of that number. The town of Old Sarum, which contains not three houses, sends two members; and the town of Manchester, which contains upwards of sixty thousand souls, is not admitted to send any. Is there any principle in these things?

Thomas Paine, *Rights of Man*

Special Advisers are temporary civil servants, and, unlike their permanent counterparts, are not expected to be politically impartial. Also, unlike professional civil servants, special advisers need not be appointed on merit. They are employed to help with government business and are popularly known as 'spin doctors'. First coined in the US, the term came into fashion in Britain under New Labour and was used exhaustively by the media, mostly to describe the behaviour of Alastair Campbell, special adviser to PM Tony Blair and perhaps the UK's most famous spin doctor to date. As Campbell demonstrated, Special Advisers can play an important and sometimes controversial role in media relations. They seek to put a government-friendly slant on news and, if they are good at their job and handle the press effectively, they have the power to influence the public by controlling what information is released and how it is presented. Their unaccountability to the same public – which did not elect them – has led many to mistrust and resent them, and some become hate figures in the popular press. When Alastair Campbell, resigned in 2003, the collective media reacted with almost as much excitement as if the Prime Minister himself had resigned.

QUOTE UNQUOTE

No woman in my time will be Prime Minister or Chancellor or Foreign Secretary – not the top jobs. Anyway I wouldn't want to be Prime Minister. You have to give yourself 100 per cent.
Margaret Thatcher, British Prime Minister 1979–1990

HEADS DOWN IN DOWNING STREET

When the IRA fired three mortar shells at Downing Street on 7 February 1991, John Major's War Cabinet kept their heads in an admirable display of sang-froid. Just as David Mellor was recounting his trip to the Gulf States, the shells were fired through the roof of a white van parked in Whitehall. Luckily for Her Majesty's government, two of them didn't go off, but the third did explode in the back garden of Number 10. Ministers ducked as the reinforced windows were blown in. The Prime Minister said, coolly, 'I think we had better start again somewhere else.' And they did. Ministers resumed the Cabinet meeting 10 minutes later in the neighbouring Cabinet Office. A record of the meeting read simply, 'A brief interruption to the war committee of the Cabinet took place.'

If it hadn't been for the loyalty of Lord Monteagle, King James I and the members of both Houses might have been wiped out at the state opening of Parliament on 5 November 1605. A small group of fervent Catholics decided to make an explosive protest against the Protestant establishment, in what became known as the Gunpowder Plot. Monteagle was the brother-in-law of one of the plotters, Francis Tresham, and on 26 October he received an anonymous letter at his Hoxton home advising him to stay away from the opening. The leader of the plotters had strictly forbidden anyone to warn their friends and family who might be attending the opening, but it is believed Tresham broke the rules. The letter was to prove the undoing of the murderous team.

Monteagle showed the letter to Robert Cecil, Earl of Salisbury and Secretary of State, and the vaults beneath the Lords were searched on 4 November. The conspirators had met there the previous night and the king's men discovered an unusual amount of firewood in one of the cellars. A further search uncovered 36 barrels of gunpowder hidden under the Lords. Guy Fawkes, one of the chief plotters, was soon tracked down and arrested. Fuses and kindling were found in his pocket and he confessed to the plot to destroy parliament.

The conspirators were put to death on 30 and 31 January 1606, after being tortured. The only one to escape this unpleasant fate was Francis Tresham, who died supposedly of an illness in the Tower of London. Some suspect that his death was arranged to cover up his part in the discovery of the plot. He had earlier tried to persuade his colleagues to postpone or even abandon their attack, so it is possible that he was involved in some counter-conspiracy with Lord Monteagle, to save not only his brother-in-law, but the king and parliament too.

Most public holidays were abolished during the reign of Charles I, but as a reminder of parliament's narrow escape, Guy Fawkes' night was enthusiastically celebrated, as it still is.

PUZZLING POLITICS

My first's in Camp David, which I first said aloud
My second's in rank, of which I was proud
My third is in Commie, who I hated to see
My whole is America's nickname for me.
Who am I?
Answer on page 153.

GONE TO THE CHILTERN HUNDREDS

It is a little-known fact that Members of Parliament are not allowed to resign. It was declared in 1623 that MPs were trusted to represent their constituencies and were not at liberty to betray that trust, so they were expected to stay put.

However, MPs wishing to make a dash for freedom can still escape the Commons by accepting the post of Bailiff of the Chiltern Hundreds. This is an 'office of profit' under the Crown. Acceptance legally disqualifies a member from continuing as an MP as his independence might be compromised by his being in the pay of the monarch.

The office is only nominally paid and generally used until another MP tenders their resignation. To this end various offices have been adopted to serve the same purpose. Currently only the Bailiff of the Chiltern Hundreds and the Steward of the Manor of Northstead are used, which means that in theory only two members may resign at once.

Fifteen Ulster Unionists got round the problem on 17 December 1985 by staggering their resignations throughout the day. Each member held one of the offices briefly before conceding to the next applicant.

The Chiltern Hundreds can be traced back to the thirteenth century. English counties were traditionally divided into 'hundreds'. Robbers notoriously used to hide in the Chiltern Hills in Buckinghamshire and a Crown Steward was appointed to maintain law and order there. The steward's duties became surplus to requirements in the sixteenth century and the office-holder no longer received benefits. John Pitt was the first to use the position as a pretext for resignation on 17 January 1751.

ASSASSINATION ATTEMPTS

When a Palestinian nationalist shot dead King Abdullah of Jordan in July 1951, his grandson Hussein was only a matter of feet away. The pair were entering the holy site of the al-Aqsa mosque in Jerusalem as the shots were fired. The life of the 16 year-old prince was saved by a medal on his uniform – worn at the insistence of his grandfather – which took the force of the bullet. The assassin was a Jerusalem tailor called Mustapha Shukri Usho. He was a member of the Arab Dynamite Squad and was motivated by a fear that Abdullah, a moderate in Western eyes, might strike a peace deal with Israel. After his father, King Talal, abdicated a year later, Hussein became king in 1953. He ruled until his death in 1999.

A BEGINNER'S GUIDE TO
ATHENIAN DEMOCRACY

For much of the fourth and fifth centuries BC, the Athenians practised a form of democracy that was purer than the Parliamentary democracies of today.

Athenians called their political system 'demokratia' – the power of the people. Citizens gathered in the 'ekklesia', or Assembly, four times every 36 days. Votes in the Assembly were normally taken in full public view, by a show of hands. The Assembly normally met on the lower slopes of the Pnyx, a small hill close to the Akropolis, and in the fourth century BC between 6,000 and 8,000 people could normally squeeze in.

A herald introduced meetings with the question, 'Who wishes to speak?' The orator Aeschines tells us that 'even the man who earns his daily bread by working at a trade' was heartily welcomed at the Assembly. In theory, every adult male was entitled to address his fellow citizens. In practice, it has to be admitted that the system leaned towards the richer city dwellers, simply because the poorer rural Athenians would have struggled to make the trip from the further reaches of the countryside. Some speakers were also more influential than others. In the 430s BC, at the height of the Peloponnesian War with the Spartans, the orator and general, Pericles, held sway in the Assembly. But if a minority threatened to dominate meetings, the majority were empowered to ostracise the leader of the minority group.

Every aspect of Athenian life, public and private, was up for discussion in the Assembly. The people chewed over issues ranging from war and finance to religion and festivals.

The Assembly's business was prepared and acted upon by the boule, or Council. This 500-strong body was broadly representative of the citizen population. Citizens over 30 were appointed by lot for a year at a time, and membership rotated. No one was allowed to serve for more than two years of his life. Rotation ensured that the Council remained in touch with public opinion. The Council split into 10 groups. Each presided over the Council for 36 days a year.

Citizens not on the Council were able to propose, in writing, subjects for its consideration, in the hope that they would be passed onto the Assembly and put to the vote.

Such privileges were denied both to the immigrant metics (resident aliens) and to the slaves. The metics were taxed but disenfranchised. Their interests were instead championed by the polemarch, an Athenian official who was appointed by lot. Women were also denied the vote.

Pericles summed up the Athenian attitude to debate: 'Rather than seeing discussion as an obstacle to action, we think it an indispensable preliminary to any wise action at all.'

DIED, RESIGNED, PROMOTED

Eighteen US Vice Presidents who didn't finish their term

George Clinton – died in office, 1812

Elbridge Gerry – died in office, 1814

John C Calhoun – resigned, 1832

John Tyler – promoted to President when, in 1841, William Harrison became the first President to die in office

Millard Fillmore – became President when Zachary Taylor died, 1850

William Rufus de Vane King – died in office, 1853

Andrew Johnson – became President when Abraham Lincoln was assassinated, 1865

Henry Wilson – died in office, 1875

Chester Alan Arthur – became President when James Garfield was assassinated, 1881

Thomas Andrews Hendricks – died in office (in his sleep), 1885

Garret Augustus Hobart – died in office, 1899

Teddy Roosevelt – became President when Leon Czolgosz was assassinated, 1901

James Schoolcraft Sherman – died in office, 1912

Calvin Coolidge – became President when Warren Harding died, 1923

Harry Truman – became President when Franklin Roosevelt died, 1945

Lyndon Johnson – became President when John F Kennedy was assassinated, 1963

Spiro Agnew – resigned, 1973

Gerald Ford – became President when Richard Nixon resigned, 1974

QUOTE UNQUOTE

Our democracy, our constitutional framework is really a kind of software for harnessing the creativity and political imagination for all of our people... The American democratic system was an early political version of Napster
Al Gore, US Vice-President 1998–2001

POLITICS IN WRITING

From the moment in which Mr Melmotte had declared his purpose of standing for Westminster in the Conservative interest, an attempt was made to drive him down the throats of the electors by clamorous assertions of his unprecedented commercial greatness. It seemed that there was but one virtue in the world, commercial enterprise - and that Melmotte was its prophet.
Anthony Trollope, *The Way We Live Now*

POLITICAL WORKAHOLICS

A few British politicians who can't get enough of their work...

The Liberal Prime Minister William Ewart Gladstone had four separate terms in office: 1868–1874, 1880–1885, 1886 and 1892–1894. He also holds the record for the longest continuous service in the House of Commons at 62 years and 206 days.

Sir Robert Walpole holds the record for longest continuous service as Prime Minister, at 20 years and 314 days.

Gwyneth Dunwoody (Labour) is the longest serving female Member of Parliament (for Crewe and Nantwich) and has been holding parliamentary functions since 1966.

The longest serving member of the House of Lords is Earl Jellicoe, who has sat since 1939.

Lord David Pitt of Hampstead (Labour) was the longest serving black Parliamentarian, from 1975–1994.

Tony Benn was the longest serving Labour MP, 1950–2001.

The odd one out is George Canning, who was Prime Minister for a shorter time than any other, holding office for just 100 days. He was ill for most of his time in office and died from pneumonia on 8 August 1827.

IT'S A SCANDAL

In 2002, journalists in Spain caught three members of the Spanish governing party looking at pornographic pictures during a debate on domestic violence in Madrid's regional parliament.

The members of the right-wing Popular Party were looking at explicit emails in the chamber when they were spotted by the hacks. They were fined between 450 and 900 euro for breaching party regulations.

I (DON'T) WANT TO HOLD YOUR HAND

Not all the members of the 'Rump' parliament who signed the Death Warrant against King Charles I appeared to have done so willingly. Thomas Hoyle killed himself in 1650 on the anniversary of Charles' execution. The death the same year of another parliament member, Rowland Wilson, was thought to be the result of his guilt and depression. Richard Ingoldsby won a pardon from the dead king's son and heir, Charles II, by claiming that Oliver Cromwell had held his hand to force him to sign.

Nineteenth-century American satirist Ambrose Bierce was the author of the incomparable work *The Devil's Dictionary*, a unique work of lexicography in which he gave vent to some very personal definitions.

POLITICS, *n.* A strife of interests masquerading as a contest of principles. The conduct of public affairs for private advantage.

POLITICIAN, *n.* An eel in the fundamental mud upon which the superstructure of organized society is reared. When he wriggles he mistakes the agitation of his tail for the trembling of the edifice. As compared with the statesman, he suffers the disadvantage of being alive.

PRESIDENCY, *n.* The greased pig in the field game of American politics.

PRESIDENT, *n.* The leading figure in a small group of men of whom – and of whom only – it is positively known that immense numbers of their countrymen did not want any of them for President.

> If that's an honor surely 'tis a greater
> To have been a simple and undamned spectator.
> Behold in me a man of mark and note
> Whom no elector e'er denied a vote! –
> An undiscredited, unhooted gent
> Who might, for all we know, be President
> By acclamation. Cheer, ye varlets, cheer –
> I'm passing with a wide and open ear!
>
> *Jonathan Fomry*

QUEEN, *n.* A woman by whom the realm is ruled when there is a king, and through whom it is ruled when there is not.

REFERENDUM, *n.* A law for submission of proposed legislation to a popular vote to learn the nonsensus of public opinion.

VOTE, *n.* The instrument and symbol of a freeman's power to make a fool of himself and a wreck of his country.

QUOTE UNQUOTE

We in America do not have government by the majority.
We have government by the majority who participate.
Thomas Jefferson, US President 1801–1809

PRESIDENTIAL SCANDALS

A decade before Grover Cleveland became President, a young widow called Maria Halpin claimed that he was the father of her illegitimate son. Although Cleveland did not deny it, the story disappeared out of the headlines after the child was put up for adoption. But Cleveland's 1884 campaign was rocked when a Buffalo newspaper got hold of the story. Cleveland finally admitted it and his opponents lampooned him with chants of 'Ma, ma, where's my pa? Gone to the White House, ha ha ha!' But it didn't seem to affect his political standing, as Cleveland won the election by a narrow 62,000 vote margin. In this case, honesty appeared to have been the best policy.

HOME TERRITORY

The remaining UK dependent territories

Alderney • Anguilla

Bermuda • British Antarctic Territory

British Indian Ocean Territory

British Virgin Islands • Cayman Islands

Falkland Islands • Gibraltar

Guernsey • Jersey • Isle of Man

Montserrat • Pitcairn Islands

Saint Helena • Sark

Sovereign Base Areas on Cyprus

South Georgia and the South Sandwich Islands

Turks and Caicos Islands

LEGLESS AT THE FUNERAL

Many politicians live to see the funeral of their own careers, but few have attended a funeral for one of their own body parts. Antonio de Santa Anna, the Mexican President who defeated the Texan rebels at the siege of the Alamo in 1836, had a funeral for his leg. The limb had been amputated below the knee during a battle with French troops in December 1838. De Santa Anna stored the leg at home while he gradually rose to power on his good leg. The spare limb was solemnly paraded through the streets of Mexico City on 26 September 1842 and de Santa Anna's loyal supporters (the people, not the crutches) buried it in a national shrine; but within two years the President had lost both his power and his buried leg, which was stolen during riots. It was never found, and when its unlucky owner died in 1876 there was no parade for the rest of him.

The last words of **William Pitt** the Younger were said to be 'Oh my country, how I leave my country!' referring to England's situation in the Napoleonic Wars. However, Disraeli later claimed he heard from a House of Commons waiter that Pitt's actual last words were: 'I think I could eat one of Bellamy's veal pies.'

Thomas Jefferson, the third US President, said: 'Is it the fourth?' It was in fact the night of the third of July, but his attendant told him it was the fourth.

'I have a terrific headache' – **Franklin D Roosevelt**

James Scott, the Duke of Monmouth, illegitimate son of Charles II, led an unsuccessful rebellion against Charles's successor, James II, and was executed after losing the Battle of Sedgemoor. The Duke addressed his executioner with these words: 'Do not hack me as you did my Lord Russell.'

President **Abraham Lincoln** said: 'She won't think anything about it.' He was watching the play *Our American Cousin* at Ford's Theatre, and the last line he heard is meant to have been: 'Well, I guess I know enough to turn you inside out, old gal – you sock-dologizing old mantrap'. During the laughter that followed, the assassin took his chance. Lincoln's wife Mary had her hand in his, and she apparently asked: 'What will Miss Harris think of my hanging on to you so?' The assassination gave rise to the famous question: 'Apart from that Mrs Lincoln, what did you think of the play?'

Leon Trotsky said to his wife on the way to the hospital after being struck on the head with an axe: 'I do not want them to undress me. I want you to undress me.'

George Washington, the first US President said: 'Have me decently buried and do not let my body be put in the vault in less than three days after I am dead.'

'Better fighting death than a slave's life' – **Emiliano Zapata**, the Mexican revolutionary

'Shoot me in the chest!' – **Benito Mussolini**, the Italian Fascist dictator, to his executioners in 1945.

Sir Walter Raleigh's last words before being beheaded on 29 October 1618 were: 'So the heart be right, it is no matter which way the head lieth.'

Prime Minister **Spencer Perceval** cried 'Murder!' as he was assassinated. His assassin, John Bellingham, ended his life with: 'I thank my God for having enabled me to meet my fate with so much fortitude and resignation.'

'Oh I'm so bored with it all' – **Winston Churchill**

'Last words are for fools who haven't said enough' – **Karl Marx**

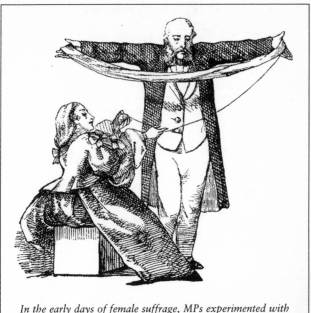

In the early days of female suffrage, MPs experimented with various ways of securing women's votes.

THE FASCINATING WORLD OF LOCAL GOVERNMENT

Who can run for local council elections in the UK?

Candidates must be British, come from a Commonwealth country or from an EU member state and be at least 21. They must be a local government elector for the local authority area or for the whole of the preceding 12 months they must have either occupied land or other premises in that area, or had their principal place of work in that area, or resided in that area or, for a parish or community council, lived in the parish or community or within three miles of it.

There are also various matters that would disqualify a hopeful candidate, including bankruptcy, electoral malpractice and recent imprisonment.

POLITICS IN POETRY

How can I, that girl standing there,
My attention fix
On Roman or on Russian
Or on Spanish politics?
Yet here's a travelled man that knows
What he talks about,
And there's a politician
That has read and thought,
And maybe what they say is true
Of war and war's alarms,
But O that I were young again
And held her in my arms!

WB Yeats, *Politics*

QUOTE UNQUOTE

Being Prime Minister is the easiest job in the world. Everyone else has an instrument to play. You just stand there and conduct.
James Callaghan, Prime Minister 1976–1979

FAMILY PLANNING

On resigning their posts, a variety of MPs have used 'spending more time with the family' as the reason. Former Tory Social Security Secretary Norman Fowler may have unwittingly started a trend when he used the line in 1990 to depart from Margaret Thatcher's government. Since his departure, a number of politicians have followed his example.

Alan Milburn resigned as Health Secretary in June 2003, his political aspirations foundering on that awkward nemesis, the family unit. 'I have already missed a good bit of my children growing up and I don't want to miss any more. It has come down to a choice between my career in politics and my life with my family,' explained Milburn.

Spin doctor Alastair Campbell announced in August 2003 his intention 'to get a life back for me and my family.' He said his family had paid a heavy price for his job.

Nor have the Tories forgotten Norman Fowler's example – even in opposition. In March 2004, David Curry resigned as shadow Secretary of State for local and devolved government 'entirely for family reasons'. He added, of course, that he had 'no political disagreements' with leader Michael Howard.

IT'S IN THE STARS

Some political leaders and their star signs.

Yasser Arafat
Star sign: Leo
Typical qualities of that sign:
Creative, jealous, enthusiastic,
bullying

Tony Blair
Star sign: Taurus
Typical qualities: Practical,
persevering, solid and stubborn

Jacques Chirac
Star sign: Sagittarius
Typical qualities:
Philosophical, boastful,
tactless, sincere

George W Bush
Star sign: Cancer
Typical qualities: Paternal,
patriotic, unforgiving,
tenacious

Vladimir Putin
Star sign: Libra
Typical qualities: Idealistic,
refined, resentful, easily
flattered

Ariel Sharon
Star sign: Pisces
Typical qualities: Impractical,
intuitive, spiteful, artistic

PUZZLING POLITICS

Which political capital am I?
SHASKA
Answer on page 153.

POLITICS IN WRITING

Josip Broz Tito was conspicuously without a particular talent except one – political. He had an exceptionally sharp and quick intelligence and a powerful and selective concentration. I observed similar characteristics in Stalin. Yet Stalin's thinking was more incisive – if somewhat slower – and showed a more acute and encompassing penetration.

Tito's qualities were manifested in both the security of his logic and the clarity of his purpose. When something was unclear to him, when he had not thought through something, he expressed himself with caution – even with confusion. That happened rarely and usually in unforeseen circumstances. His thinking so far outpaced his speech that on public occasions he would blur two or three sentences into one, with stuttering and hesitation.

Tito was in fact a poor speaker, but he could not bring himself to restrict, let alone forego, opportunities for public appearance. The writer Radovan Zogović, while still a high Communist Party official, once remarked in jest that Tito would die if he were denied the chance to speak.

Milovan Djilas,
Tito The Story from Inside

The age of Argentinian revolutionary Che Guevara when he was captured 39
and executed in the Bolivian jungle after a failed guerilla uprising

Police officer and presidential bodyguard John F Parker reported to the White House on the night of 14 April 1865 at 7pm. He was three hours late. After making his way to Ford's Theatre, he waited for the President's party to arrive before taking his seat outside the State Box. Parker had a restricted view and went to look for a better position from which to see the play, *Our American Cousin*. During the interval, Parker and Lincoln's footman, Charles Forbes, asked Francis P Burke, Lincoln's coachman, to join them for a drink in the saloon next door.

When the assassin John Wilkes Booth entered the State Box, Parker was either still in the saloon or back in his new seat. Early the following morning, Parker arrived at the police station with a woman called Lizzie Williams. He wanted her charged with prostitution, but she was released at once.

Parker was charged with neglect of duty on 1 May 1865: 'In this, that Said Parker was detailed to attend and protect the President Mr Lincoln, that while the President was at Ford's Theatre on the night of the 14 of April last, Said Parker allowed a man to enter the President's private Box and Shoot the President.' Parker was tried on 3 May, but no transcripts of the case exist, nor did the Washington newspapers cover the case. The case was dropped on 2 June.

Another of Lincoln's bodyguards, William H Crook, said of Parker: 'Had he done his duty, I believe President Lincoln would not have been murdered by Booth. Parker knew he had failed in duty. He looked like a convicted criminal the next day. He was never the same man afterward.'

Parker stayed with the police until 1868, when he was fired on 13 August for sleeping on duty. He claimed he had been ill.

THE POWER OF VETO

Queen Elizabeth I held a parliament on average only once every four years. While she advocated freedom of speech, she also made it clear that some issues were best left to her and her Privy Council.

Elizabeth didn't take kindly to parliament's request that she marry. The Queen told parliament in 1571 that they had no right to discuss issues that affected her directly.

Elizabeth vetoed laws passed by parliament on 36 occasions. When in 1585 Parliament passed a bill banning hunting, cock-fighting and bear-baiting on Sundays, she stopped the bill in its tracks. The Queen must have believed in her people's right to a good time on their day of rest.

40 *The acreage of land promised to freed slaves after the American Civil War. They were also promised a mule. They received neither*

THE RICHEST US POLITICIANS

Personal fortunes as of 2002

1. **Michael Bloomberg (Republican)**, Mayor, New York City
   Net Worth: $4.8 billion

2. **Winthrop Rockefeller (Republican)**, Lieutenant Governor,
   Arkansas. *Net Worth: $1.2 billion*

3. **B. Thomas Golisano (Independent)**, Gubernatorial Candidate,
   New York. *Net Worth: $1.1 billion*

4. **John Kerry (Democrat)**, Senator, Massachusetts
   Net Worth: $550 million

5. **Tony Sanchez (Democrat)**, Gubernatorial Candidate, Texas
   Net Worth: $500 million

6. **Amo Houghton (Republican)** Representative, New York
   Net Worth: $475 million

7. **Jon S. Corzine (Democrat)**, Senator, New Jersey
   Net Worth: $300 million

8. **Herb Kohl (Democrat)**, Senator, Wisconsin
   Net Worth: $250 million

9. **Jay Rockefeller (Democrat)**, Senator, West Virginia
   Net Worth: $200 million

10. **Mark R. Warner (Democrat)**, Governor, Virginia
    Net Worth: $200 million

SHAKESPEARE ON POLITICS

Even the most bitter political in-fighting can give way to the threat
from across the House, as Antony and Octavian discovered.

MAECENAS:
If it might please you to enforce no further
The griefs between ye; to forget them quite
Were to remember that the present need
Speaks to atone you.

LEPIDUS:
Worthily spoken, Maecenas.

ENOBARBUS:
Or, if you borrow one another's love for the
instant, you may, when you hear no more words of
Pompey, return it again. You shall have time to wrangle
in when you have nothing else to do.
Antony and Cleopatra: Act II, Scene ii

Politicians usually fall only once, but Peter Mandelson managed to do so twice. The Labour MP and confidant of Prime Minister Tony Blair was forced to resign for the second time in January 2001. He faced allegations, later disproved, of misconduct over a passport application by the Dome sponsor, the Indian Srichand Hinduja. There were claims that Mandelson had pulled strings to help Hinduja secure a UK passport after he offered to underwrite part of the Millennium Dome for £1 million while Mandelson was in charge of the project. When an inquiry by Sir Anthony Hammond QC cleared Mandelson, Downing Street said that the report showed, again, that there had been no 'passports for favours'. But Liberal Democrat MP Norman Baker described the reopened investigation as 'a whitewash whitewashing a whitewash' and as leaving 'as many unanswered questions as you'd find in a box of Trivial Pursuit.'

Mandelson's earlier brush with controversy came two days before Christmas in 1998 when he resigned just six months into his job as Secretary of State for Trade and Industry. Newspapers revealed that while Labour were in opposition, Mandelson had accepted a loan of £373,000 from fellow MP Geoffrey Robinson, to help him buy an expensive house in Notting Hill, west London. The Commons Standards and Privileges Committee would find that although Mandelson should have registered the loan, he shouldn't face punishment. Mandelson maintained his innocence throughout, but wrote in his resignation letter, 'We came to power promising to uphold the highest possible standards in public life. We have not just to do so, but we must be seen to do so.' Robinson, now Paymaster General, also resigned following the scandal.

Many have predicted a further Mandelson return to public life, despite these substantial setbacks. He seemed to disagree; after his second disgrace, he said he was also resigning to 'lead a normal life', saying 'Constant media pressure has dogged me for years.' But in a speech following his re-election in Hartlepool in 2001, he declared himself 'a fighter, not a quitter'.

POPULARITY CONTEST

On 26 March 1989 Boris Yeltsin won the highest ever personal majority for a politician. The people's deputy candidate for Moscow was elected with a margin of 4,726,112 votes. He left his closest rival trailing with 392,633 votes. The predecessor of Vladimir Putin, Yeltsin went on to become the first President of Russia after the fall of Communism.

42 *Number of years Britain's longest serving MP Tam Dalyell has spent in parliament since being elected in 1962.*

A LIFE'S WORK

World Leaders who became President for Life

Name	Country	Date of proclamation
Alexandre Sabès dit Pétion	Haiti	1808
José Gaspar Rodríguez de Francia	Paraguay	1820
Yuan Shikai	China	1915
Josip Broz Tito	Yugoslavia	1963
Sukarno	Indonesia	1963
François Duvalier	Haiti	1964
Hastings Kamuzu Banda	Malawi	1971
Jean-Bédel Bokassa	Central African Republic	1972
Francisco Macías Nguema	Equatorial Guinea	1972
Ferdinand Marcos	Philippines	1973
Habib Bourguiba	Tunisia	1975
Idi Amin	Uganda	1976
Lennox Sebe	Ciskei	1983
Saparmurat Niyazov	Turkmenistan	1999

QUOTE UNQUOTE

*I must remind the right honourable gentleman
that a monologue is not a decision.*
Clement Attlee, Prime Minister 1945–1951, to Winston Churchill

POLITICS IN WRITING

As soon as Dawn appeared, fresh and rosy-fingered, Odysseus' son got up from his bed and put his clothes on. He slung a sharp sword from his shoulder, bound a stout pair of sandals on his glistening feet and strode from his bedroom looking like a god. He at once gave orders to the clear-voiced criers to call the long-haired Achaeans to Assembly. The heralds cried their summons and the people quickly gathered. When all had arrived and the Assembly was complete, Telemachus himself set out for the meeting-place, bronze spear in hand, escorted only by two hunting dogs. Athene endowed him with such supernatural grace that all eyes were turned on him in admiration when he came up. The elders made way for him as he took his father's seat.

Homer, *The Odyssey*

It is impossible to obtain a conviction for sodomy from an English jury. Half of them don't believe that it can physically be done, and the other half are doing it.

When I am abroad I always make it a rule never to criticise or attack the Government of my country. I make up for lost time when I am at home.

The best argument against democracy is a five-minute conversation with the average voter.

On Clement Attlee: A sheep in sheep's clothing.

Success is the ability to go from failure to failure without losing your enthusiasm.

Personally, I like short words and vulgar fractions.

On Irish House Rule: The Times is speechless and takes three columns to express its speechlessness.

Out of intense complexities, intense simplicities emerge.

Everyone has a right to pronounce foreign words as he chooses.

Mr Gladstone read Homer for fun, which I thought served him right.

I like pigs. Dogs look up to us. Cats look down on us. Pigs treat us as equals.

I am ready to meet my Maker. Whether my Maker is prepared for the great ordeal of meeting me is another matter.

This is not the end. It is not even the beginning of the end. But it is, perhaps, the end of the beginning.

Everyone has his day and some days last longer than others

Lady Astor to Churchill: 'Sir, if you were my husband, I would flavour your coffee with poison.' *Churchill to Lady Astor:* 'Madam, if you were my wife, I would drink it.'

On Ramsay MacDonald: I remember when I was a child, being taken to the celebrated Barnum's Circus, which contained an exhibition of freaks and monstrosities, but the exhibit on the programme which I most desired to see was the one described as 'The Boneless Wonder'. My parents judged that the spectacle would be too demoralising and revolting for my youthful eye and I have waited 50 years to see the The Boneless Wonder sitting on the Treasury Bench.

On Clement Attlee: A modest man, who has much to be modest about.

I am never going to have anything more to do with politics or politicians. When this war is over I shall confine myself entirely to writing and painting.

---

44   *Year, in the twentieth century, the Daily Mail became the first transoceanic newspaper*

I have a bream...

ASSASSINATION ATTEMPTS

A New York bartender called John Schrank fired at Theodore Roosevelt in October 1912 as he was heading for a campaign rally in Milwaukee, Wisconsin. The bullet penetrated Roosevelt's eyeglasses case as well as his 50-page speech. It fractured his fourth rib and became embedded in his chest. Undeterred, Roosevelt made his speech before going to hospital. Although he soon got better, he lost the November election. Schrank, a German immigrant, was sent to a mental institution after he claimed former President William McKinley had instructed him to kill Roosevelt in a dream. He was sentenced to life in an asylum. Roosevelt died in 1919 with the bullet still lodged in his chest.

Length in minutes of the shortest Budget speech given by Benjamin Disraeli 45
in 1867

The national dishes of each of the newest EU members, and what they might drink with it

Cyprus
Kleftiko (oven-baked lamb) and mezedes (dips, salads and other appetisers); Mavro, Xinisteri, Opthalmo and Muscat (wines).

The Czech Republic
Knedlo-zelo-vepro (dumplings, sauerkraut and roast pork); beer

Estonia
Verevorst (blood sausages) and vere pannkoogid (blood pancakes); Vana Tallinn liqueur

Hungary
Pörkölt (stew, also known as goulash); pálinka (brandy)

Latvia
Cukas galerts (pork in aspic) and pelmeni (eastern European ravioli); Riga Black Balsam (a thick, jet-black alcoholic beverage)

Lithuania
Cepelinai (a zeppelin-shaped parcel of potato dough with cheese, meat or mushrooms in the centre); beer

Malta
Pastizzi (savoury cheese pastries), timpana (a macaroni, cheese and egg pie) and fenek (rabbit); wine.

Poland
Bigos (sauerkraut and meat) and barszcz (beetroot soup); tea and vodka

Slovakia
Bryndzové halusky (gnocchi with a thick sheep's cheese sauce and crumbled grilled bacon); slivovice (plum brandy)

Slovenia
Burek, (a layered cheese, meat or even apple pie); Terran (wine)

PRISON POLITICS

When the US politician, Knott County Judge-Executive Donnie Newsome, was sentenced to more than two years in prison in 2004 for buying votes, he was allowed to continue to hold his post from his cell.

Newsome had been in jail since his conviction in October 2003 when a federal judge said he was a danger to the community. There had been allegations of witness tampering during his trial, but a Kentucky state law, which stipulated that convicted felons could not be removed until their appeals were exhausted, meant that he was able to carry on working as the top county administrator from prison.

Newsome had been charged in connection with election fraud, following an FBI investigation into the 1998 primary election. He was convicted of buying and conspiring to buy votes.

46 *Year, in the 1900s, when Italy voted by referendum to abolish their royal family*

KNOWING YOUR LEFT FROM YOUR RIGHT

Few terms are used as often as 'left' and 'right' in British politics, but their origin is in fact French. During the early revolutionary era in France, left and right referred to the seating arrangements in the French legislative bodies. On the right of the Speaker sat the aristocracy, on the left the commoners. 'The Right' was therefore associated with the interests of the aristocracy and royalty under the Ancien Régime (the 'old order').

Support for laissez-faire capitalism has not always been the prerogative of 'The Right'. As part of a narrow political franchise before the The French Revolution, 'The Left' represented chiefly the interests of the bourgeoisie, the rising capitalist class.

PUZZLING POLITICS

Who am I?
M + backward beer
Answer on page 153.

THE DEFINITION OF NEPOTISM

For those seeking political office in Iraq under Saddam Hussein, it helped to be a member of his family. During his presidency, Saddam held the record for the most family appointments to positions of power. His half-brother, Barzan Ibrahim was ambassador to the UN. A second half-brother, Watban Ibrahim, was Minister of the Interior. A third, Sabaoni Ibrahim, was Chief of General Security. Saddam Kamal Hussein, the leader's son-in-law, was Commander of the Presidential Guard. Saddam's sons Uday and Qusay both held various offices of state and Uday was expected to be his father's heir. But family ties could also be a disadvantage. Kamal Hussein was executed in 1996 after he defected. And when things turned bad for Saddam in 2003, family members became the target: Uday and Qusay were killed in a gun battle with American troops after the invasion of Iraq by allied forces.

VOTED OUT

The Athenian Cleisthenes came up with a negative form of election in 508 BC; citizens could vote for the politician they most wanted to see exiled. Votes were written on broken pots called 'ostraka', which gave rise to the word 'ostracise'. As long as 6,000 votes were cast altogether, the 'candidate' who received the most votes would be banished for 10 years, although without losing his property or citizen status.

*Sir, you have a right to speak, but the House has
a right to judge whether they will hear you.*
Earl of Wilmington, Prime Minister 1742–1743

KEEPING IT IN THE FAMILY

Families that have produced more than one US President:

Father and son:
John Adams (1797–1801)
John Quincy Adams
(1825–1829)

Grandfather and grandson:
William Henry Harrison
(1841–1841)
Benjamin Harrison (1889–1893)

Fifth cousins:
Theodore Roosevelt
(1901–1909)
Franklin D Roosevelt
(1933–1945)

Father and son
George Bush (1989–1993)
George W Bush (2001–)

...and some near misses:

In 1968 *Robert F Kennedy* ran for the Democratic candidacy, winning primaries in California, Indiana, South Dakota and Nebraska, but was shot dead before the election. If his candidacy had succeeded, he and John F Kennedy would have been the first brothers to be President.

Bob Dole won the Republican nomination for President in 1996. Three years later his wife Elizabeth Dole joined a committee running for the GOP nomination, making them the first husband and wife to run for President in US history.

WHIGS AND TORIES

These terms were originally insults written in 1679 by an anonymous pamphleteer during the exclusion crisis. The dispute was about whether Charles II's brother James, Duke of York, of Roman Catholic faith, should succeed to the throne. Tory comes from the Irish word 'toraidehe' meaning outlaw or robber. Tories were seen as Papist rebels because they supported James. Whig meant Scottish Presbyterian, particularly a Covenanter, and applied to those who claimed the power of excluding the heir from the throne. The origin of the word is not clear – some have it as meaning a horse thief, and 'whig-maleerie' is an old Scottish word meaning a silly idea.

POLITICS IN WRITING

There is no end to suffering, Glaucon, for our cities, and none, I suspect, for the human race, unless either philosophers become kings in our cities, or the people who are now called kings and rulers become, in the truest and most complete sense of the word, philosophers – unless there is this amalgamation of political power and philosophy, with all those people whose inclination is to pursue one or other exclusively being forcibly prevented from doing so. Otherwise there is not the remotest chance of the political arrangements we have described coming about – to the extent that they can – or seeing the light of day.

Plato, *The Republic*

PRESIDENTIAL SCANDALS

Before becoming President, the five-star general Dwight Eisenhower is alleged to have had an affair with his Irish driver, Kay Summersby, during the Second World War in Europe. Eisenhower allegedly intended to divorce his wife Mamie and marry Summersby. But his superior, General George Marshall, threatened to throw him out of the army and ruined his plan. The story was exposed in 1975, when Summersby wrote a book entitled *Past Forgetting: My Love Affair with Dwight D. Eisenhower.* Eisenhower is perhaps most famous for overseeing the 1944 D-Day landings in Normandy.

WORLD'S FIRST FEMALE
PRIME MINISTERS AND PRESIDENTS

1. Sirimavo Bandaranaike – *PM, Sri Lanka, 1960–1965, 1970–1977, 1994–2000*

2. Indira Gandhi – *PM, India, 1966–1977, 1980–1984*

3. Golda Meir – *PM, Israel, 1969–1974*

4. Maria Estela Peron – *President, Argentina, 1974–1976*

5. Elisabeth Domitien – *PM, Central African Republic, 1975–1976*

6. Margaret Thatcher – *PM, UK, 1979–1990*

7. Dr Maria Lurdes Pintasilgo – *PM, Portugal, 1979–1980*

8. Lilia Guila Tejada – *PM, Bolivia, 1979–1980*

9. Mary Eugenia Charles – *PM, Dominica, 1980–1995*

10. Vigdis Finnbogadottir – *President, Iceland, 1980–1996*

When journalist Andrew Gilligan alleged in 2003 that the government had 'sexed' up a dossier on Iraq, he set in motion a political scandal that was escalated by the suicide of weapons expert David Kelly and sparked the Hutton inquiry. Here is an outline of the judge's findings...

Lord Hutton was appointed to head the inquiry, which opened on 1 August 2003. Hutton interviewed over 70 witnesses during 22 days of hearings.

Dr David Kelly
Hutton believed that Kelly did not tell Gilligan that the government probably knew or suspected that the claim that Iraq could be ready to launch weapons of mass destruction in 45 minutes was wrong when it drew up the dossier. But meeting 'unauthorised' and in breach of Civil Service code of procedure.

Tony Blair, *Prime Minister*
Cleared of persuading intelligence officials to exaggerate the dossier's content. Allegations that the government had inserted intelligence knowing it to be wrong or questionable were 'unfounded'. But it was possible that those in charge of drawing up the dossier could have been 'subconsciously influenced' by Blair's desire to have a strongly worded dossier. *Remained Prime Minister.*

Alastair Campbell, *Director of Communications*
Made it clear nothing to be inserted into the dossier that went against the wishes of the Joint Intelligence Committee. Gilligan's allegation that

Downing Street probably knew or suspected the 45 minutes claim was wrong 'unfounded'. *Resigned during the inquiry but cited personal reasons.*

Gavyn Davies, *former Chairman of the BBC board of governors*
BBC governors should not have relied on assurances from BBC management over reliability of Gilligan's report. *Resigned.*

Greg Dyke, former BBC Director General
BBC's editorial system defective. BBC managers should have checked the detail of Gilligan's report. *Resigned the day after Hutton delivered his findings.*

John Scarlett, *Chairman of the Joint Intelligence Committee (responsible for overseeing publication of report)*
There to ensure that the dossier's contents were consistent with what it believed to be the truth. But it 'cannot be ruled out' that Blair's wishes for a strong dossier may have influenced Scarlett.

Andrew Gilligan, *Defence Correspondent, BBC Radio 4's Today programme*
Allegation that Campbell had 'sexed up' the dossier baseless. Criticised the allegation that the government probably knew that the 45-minute claim was wrong.

POLITICS IN WRITING

Since 1970, the ordinary people of the Arab world had been without a personality around whom they could rally. Many during the late 1980s were only too happy to latch on to Osama, the charismatic young Islamite who was both financing and leading the fight to oust the Soviet Union from Afghanistan. Ironically his story was one that also suited all the varied political shades of the region. In the Middle East's Islamic democracies and more extreme dictatorships he was portrayed as the pious Osama bin Laden, who had turned his back on the trappings of wealth to take up a noble cause. The oil-rich monarchies of the Gulf had a different angle. There he was held up as an example of how the Arab world's nouveau riche had not, after all, lost their religious beliefs.

Either way, Osama was Islam's rising star during the late 1980s. In offices and shops around the region, amid traditional Koranic inscriptions and the obligatory touched-up and sanitised photograph of one's leader, those well informed and politically aware now hung a photograph of Osama bin Laden.

Adam Robinson, *Bin Laden, Behind the mask of the terrorist*

A GOOD DEED UNDONE

The Canadian equivalent of No 10 Downing Street is 24 Sussex Drive. Unlike his British counterpart, however, the first Canadian Prime Minister to move in insisted on paying the rent. Louis St Laurent was his country's 12th Prime Minister, and was referred to as 'Uncle Louis'. All prime ministers followed suit until Pierre Trudeau realised he was the one who made the rules, and un-paid his rent in 1971. Trudeau also once pulled off a pirouette behind the back of Queen Elizabeth II.

IT'S YOUR BIRTHDAY

Political leaders and their famous birthday pals

12 February	Abraham Lincoln (1809) and Charles Darwin (1809)
2 March	Mikhail Gorbachev (1931) and Tom Wolfe (1931)
11 March	Harold Wilson (1916) and Rupert Murdoch (1931)
29 March	John Major (1943) and Eric Idle (1943)
6 May	Tony Blair (1953) and Maximilien Robespierre (1758)
29 May	John F Kennedy (1917) and Charles II (1630)
6 July	George W Bush (1946) and Sylvester Stallone (1946)
18 July	Nelson Mandela (1918) and Napoleon V Bonaparte (1862)
27 August	Lyndon B Johnson (1908) and Sir Donald Bradman (1908)
7 October	Vladimir Putin (1952) and Elijah Muhammad (1896)

BY ANY OTHER NAME

Some politician's nicknames

Silvio Berlusconi	*The Knight*
Tony Blair	*Teflon Tony, Bambi*
Gordon Brown	*The Iron Chancellor*
George W Bush	*Dubya, Junior, King George, Commander in Thief*
Stephen Byers	*The Limpet*
Jacques Chirac	*The Bulldozer*
Bill Clinton	*Slick Willie*
Calvin Coolidge	*Cautious Cal, Silent Cal*
Iain Duncan Smith	*The Quiet Man*
Sonia Gandhi	*The Sphinx*
William Gladstone	*The Grand Old Man*
Michael Heseltine	*Tarzan*
Thomas Jefferson	*The Red Fox*
Roy Jenkins	*The Duke of Burgundy*
Neil Kinnock	*The Welsh Windbag*
Abraham Lincoln	*Honest Abe, The Illinois Ape*
Ken Livingstone	*Red Ken*
David Lloyd George	*The Welsh Wizard*
Harold Macmillan	*Supermac*
Peter Mandelson	*Mandy, The Prince of Darkness*

PUZZLING POLITICS

Which US President am I?
TOCLN
Answer on page 153.

STAMP DUTY

The privilege of Free Franks, or Franking, was introduced in 1652 as a way for Members of Parliament and certain state officials to send their letters free of charge. The letters had to be work-related, of course, but all that members were required to do was write their name and the word 'free' or 'frank' in the corner of the letter and close it with their seal. The government-owned post office began to lose a great deal of money. MPs, Lords and Clergy started sending private letters and giving signed, empty letters to family or friends to use. A letter from Carmarthen to London in March 1760 read: 'I have taken the liberty of inclosing a frank to save the expence of postage when you will be pleas'd to write to, Sir, your most humble servant'. Measures were introduced to curb members' enthusiasm for the system. They were required to write their full name and the date. But post office officials were still not allowed to open mail. The privilege was eventually cancelled with the introduction of 'Penny Postage' in 1840.

VICIOUS VICTORY

The Westminster election of 1784 was rowdy. Charles James Fox was up against Sir Cecil Wray, his fellow member for Westminster. The pair had been close friends before Fox sided with his own arch-enemy Lord North to form a coalition government in 1783. The government candidate, Admiral Lord Hood, was the third contender.

Polling lasted 40 days, in itself a recipe for a small political war. Erskine May wrote that it was 'disgraced throughout by scenes of drunkenness, tumult, and violence – and by the coarsest libels and lampoons'. There was rioting and battles took place between the supporters of Fox and Hood. The latter canvassed using French and Spanish ensigns he had taken at war. When a police constable was killed, both sides blamed the other.

A week before the poll closed Pitt the Younger, the leader of the Tories whom Fox had vigorously opposed, was given Freedom of the City of London. On his return to Westminster from a City dinner, he was met by hordes of his supporters. As they passed the Whig Party's HQ in Brooke's club on St James's Street they demanded the windows be lit up in Pitt's honour.

This did not go down well with the Whigs. Club servants were sent out into the streets armed with sticks and other weapons. The club members themselves hurled missiles from the windows. Pitt managed to escape to White's club, the Tory base, but his carriage was smashed to pieces. Fox was accused of masterminding the whole affair, but he had an alibi: 'I was in bed with Mrs Armistead – who is ready to substantiate the fact on oath.'

Hood won the first seat with 6,694 votes. Fox (6,234) squeezed into the second ahead of Sir Cecil (5,998). However, the fight resumed when Sir Cecil demanded a recount. The High Bailiff conducted a long and drawn out scrutiny of the votes, but after eight months of recounting, Parliament accepted the original result. Meanwhile Fox secured a seat in the far-flung constituency of Kirkwall Burghs, a place he had never visited

POLITICS IN POETRY

Here richly, and with ridiculous display,
The Politician's corpse was laid away.
While all of his acquaintance sneered and slanged
I wept: for I had wished to see him hanged.

Hilaire Belloc, *Epitaph on the Politician Himself*

*In his lesser-known early career, Lincoln would
stare for hours on end at the salon's slogan:*
Hairdressing of the people, by the people, for the people

RULES OF THE HOUSE

The phrase 'Speaker's Chop' was first used in the nineteenth century and referred to the break in the House's business of the day that was created so the Speaker could grab a bite to eat. This was because the Speaker had to remain in his chair as long as the Commons were sitting. And as no food is allowed in the Chamber, and there were no Deputy Speakers to take his place at this time, the Speaker's Chop was the only chance the unfortunate man had to nip out for a little sustenance. These days the Speaker can be replaced by a deputy at any time, so the term 'Speaker's Chop' has become redundant. The deputy speaker's formal title is Chairman of Ways and Means (referring to the provision of revenue to meet national expenditure by way of 'charges upon the people', taxation being the principal means) and he also presides over the Budget. There are two deputy Chairmen of Ways and Means who step in when both the Speaker and his deputy are unavailable.

20TH CENTURY US PRESIDENTS

William McKinley, *1897–1901* ....Republican
Theodore Roosevelt, *1901–1909* ....Republican
William H. Taft, *1909–1913*...Republican
Woodrow Wilson, *1913–1921* ....Democrat
Warren Harding, *1921–1923* ....Republican
Calvin Coolidge, *1923–1929* ....Republican
Herbert Hoover, *1929–1933*..Republican
Franklin D. Roosevelt, *1933–1945* ....Democrat
Harry Truman, *1945–1953*...Democrat
Dwight Eisenhower, *1953–1961* ....Republican
John F. Kennedy, *1961–1963* ....Democrat
Lyndon Johnson, *1963–1969*...Democrat
Richard Nixon, *1969–1974*..Republican
Gerald Ford, *1974–1977* ....Republican
Jimmy Carter, *1977–1981*...Democrat
Ronald Reagan, *1981–1989* ....Republican
George HW Bush, *1989–1993*..Republican
William J Clinton, *1993–2001* ....Democrat
George W Bush, *2001–*...Republican

QUOTE UNQUOTE

You can't get rich in politics unless you're a crook.
Harry S Truman, US President, 1945–1953

DEAD MAN STANDING

In the US elections of 2000, the people of Missouri elected a dead man as their senator. Governor Mel Carnahan died in a plane crash less than a month before the public went to the polls. However, state law made it impossible for his name to be struck off the ballot papers, and loyal, or perhaps forgetful, voters gave Democrat Carnahan 50.5% of the vote, beating rival John Ashcroft. Carnahan's widow, Jean, announced before polling day that she would accept the appointment by the acting governor to the Senate should her late husband oust the incumbent Ashcroft. As the votes began to stack up in Mel's favour, she said: 'You have stayed the course; you have kept the faith; you have carried our hopes and dreams. Lincoln never saw his nation made whole again. Susan B Anthony never cast a vote. Martin Luther King never finished his mountaintop journey. My husband's journey was cut short, too. And for reasons we don't understand, the mantle has now fallen upon us.' Carnahan filled the vacancy left by her husband until she lost the election for the rest of the term to Republican Jim Talent.

Age of Mao Zedong when he became leader of his newly declared People's 55
Republic of China in 1949

GIVE YOURSELF A PAY RISE

Since 1971 the independent review body, the Senior Salaries Review body (SSRB) have made recommendations on MPs' pay. The final decision rests with the House itself. Here is a selection of MPs' salaries since 1911, when parliament first decided that MPs should be given an official salary...

1911	£400
1937	£600
1954	£1,250
1964	£3,250
1975	£5,750
1977	£6,270
1979	£9,450
1981	£13,950
1983	£15,308
1985	£16,904
1987	£18,500
1989	£24,107
1991	£28,970
1993	£30,854
1995	£33,189
1996	£34,085
1998	£45,066
1999	£47,008
2001	£51,822
2002	£55,118
2003	£56,358
2004	£57,485

WRITING ABOUT POLITICS

Peter Riddell, columnist for *The Times*, on political journalism:
Writing about politics is 40 per cent hard work, 40 per cent good judgement and 20 per cent having a nose for when something is about to happen (you can call it good luck). The three are linked. The more you talk to people, the better the chance you have to pick up new developments and changes in mood. The two big risks in political journalism are a lack of proportion and a lack of detachment. The dangers are exaggeration and excessive partisanship. You need to be close, but not too close. All politicians spin, they always have. The tricky task is to weave your way through the propaganda. The fun of political journalism is that you have a unique insight into how we are governed: government and opposition, ministers and civil servants. And most of the time it is cock-up, rather than conspiracy.

Adults they may be, but the behaviour of MPs is subject to so many restrictions that some might feel as if they never left school.

Briefcases are forbidden in the chamber, as is the reading of newspapers or other reading material not connected with the issue at hand. Members should not have their hands in their pockets in the House. Such an offence is likely to be recorded and the incident brought up again and again to the offender's eternal shame. The Tory MP Andrew Robathan, for example, is still badgered about a 'hands in' episode on December 1994.

Members are also now asked to turn off their mobile phones in the Commons, although they can be set to silent ring. In December 2003, the Conservative MP for North West Norfolk, Henry Bellingham, was ejected from the House by Speaker Michael Martin when he was caught using a mobile phone complete with camera. The account of the incident read as follows:

Mr Speaker: 'Order. The hon. Member for North-West Norfolk is using a camera.'

Mr Bellingham: 'It is a mobile phone.'

Mr Speaker: The hon. Member should not be using a mobile phone. I ask him to leave the Chamber.'

At no point was Bellingham recorded as shouting: 'I'M ON THE PHONE.'

QUOTE UNQUOTE

There are two problems in my life. The political ones are insoluble and the economic ones are incomprehensible.
Sir Alec Douglas-Home, Prime Minister, 1963–1964

IT'S A SCANDAL

In December 1825, the City experienced a devastating crash and a young Benjamin Disraeli – the future Prime Minister – found himself thousands of pounds in debt. Disraeli was a law apprentice between the ages of 17 and 20. At the same time he had tried to make money by buying and selling shares, but ended up with heavy losses instead. Disraeli spent years avoiding those he owed money to and took to writing to pay off his debts. In his first novel, *Vivian Grey,* anonymously written in 1826, he so closely parodied his friends and associates that he was threatened more than once with a duel. Disraeli made four attempts to get into parliament between 32 and 35, but failed on each occasion. He was finally elected for the first time as MP for Maidstone at the General Election of July 1837 that followed the accession of Victoria to the throne.

'Risk' is not the only political board game. Here are a few others:

Banana Republic – A tactical game of manipulation involving bribery to obtain votes. Tools of control include journalists, bodyguards and hired assasins.

Candidate – You have to secure the support of the American people state by state to become President. There are always worries about fundraising and dirty tricks from opponents.

Consensus – Based on the Electoral College system. Target voter interest groups to secure enough support for election.

Corruption – The name of this game is bribery. Underhand tactics are required to get the good contracts and most profits.

Democrazy – Players have to try to pass laws that are beneficial to themselves with the consent of their fellow players.

Die Macher – Once your favourite party has been selected you have to try to lead it to victory in order to rule the Reichstag.

Election – Manipulation and canvassing are necessary means of ensuring your term in office.

Koalition – Being elected into the European Union calls for party scandals, press campaigns and filthy intrigues to bring about the downfall of your opponents.

Landslide – In the race for the White House, players must secure as big a majority as possible to win.

Mr President – A card game requiring players to amass total support from all the US States to secure victory. Hone your skills of persuasion.

Politics – When trying to become the American President, you have to control votes and use slander and rumours as your main weapons against opposition.

Road to the White House – Another race to rule the US, this game requires you to balance finances, image and tactics if you are to fulfil your dream of presidency.

QUOTE UNQUOTE

There are lots of people I've encouraged and helped to get into the House of Commons. Looking at them now, I'm not at all sure it was a wise thing to do.
James Callaghan, Prime Minister 1976–1979

PUPPET POWER

Margaret Thatcher appeared as a Reagan groupie, John Major as a grey man who only ate peas. Kenneth Baker was a slug, and a mini David Steel popped out from David Owen's pocket. The television programme 'Spitting Image' lampooned politicians from 1984 to 1996 when viewing figures suggested the satirical show had lost its bite. At its height, up to 15 million tuned in to get their Sunday evening fix of politicians being humiliated. Other memorable features included Roy Hattersley's saliva problem and Neil Kinnock's role as Kinnochio. Anticipating a possible return of the programme, John Lloyd, one of the original producers, said in 2004: 'The way things are happening at the moment is much more interesting and dangerous. You've got Michael Howard running the Tories and Geoff Hoon – oh, what a joy.' He added, 'It's not that Spitting Image has any better answers to all these terrible things that are going on in the world. But it's a thoughtful and amusing way of looking at stuff.'

PUZZLING POLITICS

It is well known that Gordon Brown is after the job of Prime Minister, but what is his quickest way of achieving the top spot?

By changing one letter at a time, turn BLAIR into BROWN.
Answer on page 153.

POLITICS IN WRITING

When I was selected, Matthew Parris, who was an MP in Derbyshire before becoming a seer of Fleet Street (and especially of the Spectator), wrote me a letter. As usual, he showed profound psychological insight. 'All Tory candidates in safe seats have a moment of panic when they think they are about to be beaten by the Liberal Democrats. Don't worry. It won't happen.'

Somehow my sang-froid is draining away today, and Parris's advice seems less and less convincing. They are everywhere these Liberal Democrats, like self-seeding yellow poppies: kindly, principled, reasonable, and sometimes just a little bit maddening.

You can always tell the Liberal Democrats, says Chris Scott, because they refuse to say how they are going to vote. 'I'm so sorry,' they say, with an air of slight holiness, 'but that is between me and the ballot box'; or 'That is my business. I am afraid I never tell anyone how I vote, and I do not propose to start with you young man.'

Boris Johnson, *Friends, Voters, Countrymen*

Known as the Stars and Stripes, the American flag shows 50 stars and 13 stripes. The stars represent the 50 states, while the stripes represent the original states. When it was first flown in 1777 the flag had only 13 stars to match the 13 stripes. When Vermont and then Kentucky joined the union in 1791 and 1792, a star and a stripe were added for each. But as more states signed up, it was clear the flag would become somewhat crowded. Every state couldn't have a stripe, so in 1818 the number of stripes reverted to 13.

The flag inspired the poet and lawyer Francis Scott Key to compose the words of 'The Star-spangled Banner' – now the national anthem – in 1814. First flown on 3 August 1777, from Fort Stanwix (where the city of Rome now is in New York), the Stars and Stripes came under attack three days later at the Battle of Oriskany. It was first carried into battle on 11 September 1777 at Brandywine, and was first flown over foreign territory on 28 January 1778 at Nassau in the Bahamas, during the War of Independence. The French admiral LaMotte Piquet gave the flag its first foreign salute off Quiberon Bay on 13 February 1778.

George Washington, the first President, had this to say of the flag's symbolism: 'We take the stars from Heaven, the red from our mother country, separating it by white stripes, thus showing that we have separated from her, and the white stripes shall go down to posterity representing Liberty.'

Captain William Driver gave the flag its other nickname, 'Old Glory', on 10 August 1831.

The flag is the third oldest National Standard in the world and Americans celebrate Flag Day on 14 June, the date on which Congress officially authorised the flag.

SHAKESPEARE ON POLITICS

History tends to smile kindly on political winners – they can rewrite the history books.

OCTAVIUS CAESAR:
Go with me to my tent, where you shall see
How hardly I was drawn into this war,
How calm and gentle I proceeded still
In all my writings. Go with me, and see
What I can show in this.

Antony and Cleopatra, Act V, Scene i

QUOTE UNQUOTE

I am more or less happy when being praised, not very comfortable when being abused, but I have moments of uneasiness when being explained.
Arthur Balfour, Prime Minister, 1902–1905

A STEP IN THE RIGHT DIRECTION

To become the Prime Minister, it might help to become President first of the Oxford Union. Prime Ministers Gladstone, Salisbury, Asquith, McMillan and Heath were all Presidents of the Oxford Union.

The presidency does not guarantee premiership, however. Oxford Presidents Tony Benn, Michael Foot and William Hague never quite made it to Number 10. Hague even earned the dubious honour of becoming the first Tory leader since Austin Chamberlain not to become Prime Minister. As for Michael Heseltine, another President, his failure to reach Number 10 was not for the want of trying. He was elected President after he completed his finals, and stayed on for an extra term to attend to his duties.

STICKS AND STONES MAY BREAK MY BONES...

Teddy Roosevelt has the distinction of being the only president to get into a fight over being called Four Eyes. When a drunken gunman tried to provoke Roosevelt by referring so rudely to his spectacles in the bar of a hotel in Dakota in 1884, the future President reportedly tried to laugh off the insult. Roosevelt took a seat, but the drunkard continued to harass him, testing Roosevelt's conflict resolution skills to the limit. He decided on what now might be called a surgical strike. As he explained in his autobiography, he 'struck him and hard with my right fist just to one side of the point of his jaw, hitting with my left as I straightened out and then again with my right... when he went down he struck the corner of the bar with his head.' It had the required effect, though the episode sits uneasily with Roosevelt's view that the leader of the US should be a 'steward of the people'.

It was a bad time for Teddy, as during the year of his saloon showdown, his first wife, Alice Lee Roosevelt, and his mother died on the same day. Roosevelt passed much of the next couple of years driving cattle and hunting big game on his ranch in the Badlands of Dakota Territory. Nevertheless he went on to become the youngest ever president at the age of 42 in 1901.

Well, I think if you say you're going to do something and don't do it, that's trustworthiness.

Arbolist... Look up the word. I don't know, maybe I made it up. Anyway, it's an arbo-tree-ist, somebody who knows about trees.

The French have no word for entrepreneur.

I understand that the unrest in the Middle East creates unrest throughout the region.

My administration has been calling upon all the leaders in the Middle East to do everything they can to stop the violence, to tell the different parties involved that peace will never happen.

Our nation must come together to unite.

These terrorist acts and, you know, the responses have got to end in order for us to get the framework – the groundwork – not framework, the groundwork to discuss a framework for peace, to lay the – all right.

Over the long term, the most effective way to conserve energy is by using energy more efficiently.

I'm not very analytical. You know I don't spend a lot of time thinking about myself, about why I do things.

I am mindful not only of preserving executive powers for myself, but for predecessors as well.

Redefining the role of the United States from enablers to keep the peace to enablers to keep the peace from peacekeepers is going to be an assignment.

Natural gas is hemispheric. I like to call it hemispheric in nature because it is a product that we can find in our neighbourhoods.

The reason I believe in a large tax cut is because it's what I believe.

I've coined new words, like 'misunderstanding' and 'Hispanically'.

The thing that's important for me is to remember what's the most important thing.

This foreign policy stuff is a little frustrating.

I admit it, I am not one of the great linguists.

And so, in my State of the – my State of the Union – or State – my speech to the nation, whatever you want to call it, speech to the nation – I asked Americans to give 4,000 years – 4,000 hours over the next – the rest of your life – of service to America. That's what I asked – 4,000 hours.

Tony Benn loved to show off his version of an economic cycle.

QUOTE UNQUOTE

*It is hard to believe a man is telling the truth when you know that
you would lie if you were in his place.*
H L Mencken, US newspaper editor

ASSASSINATION ATTEMPTS

More than one attempt was made on the life of Charles de Gaulle, not
least because he angered anti-independence factions when he began to
favour Algerian independence. On one occasion de Gaulle was
travelling in a motorcade with his wife on the outskirts of Paris in
August 1963 when gunmen opened fire. Bullets punctured tires and
shattered the rear window, but the couple survived unharmed. On
getting out of the car, de Gaulle exclaimed: 'They really are bad shots.'

'That night in the surgery there were three patients, two of whom paid him the three-and-sixpenny fee. The third promised to return and settle up on Saturday. He had, in his first day's practice, earned the sum of ten and six.' AJ Cronin's novel *The Citadel* tells the tale of 1920s health care in Britain when patients paid to get better. It took the vision of the Labour Health Secretary Aneurin Bevan to introduce a system of free healthcare for all. Building on Lloyd George's health insurance system of 1911, the National Health Service Act 1946 was brought into effect in 1948 after some stiff opposition from doctors.

Hospitals were nationalised and only the Chancellor of the Exchequer found himself out of pocket. Doctors' pay actually increased and those patients who could afford it still had the option of private health care. Bevan said at the launch of the service: 'We shall never have all we need. Expectations will always exceed capacity. The service must always be changing, growing and improving – it must always appear inadequate.'

SHOCK TACTICS

A nipple made an unexpected appearance in the build up to the European Parliament elections of 2004. A short film designed to encourage voters to turn out backfired when the opening shot of a baby breast-feeding was deemed too shocking for British audiences. The message was: 'You have been voting since you were born: don't stop now – European elections, June 10.' The promotional video was sent back to Strasbourg for editing and the film, minus the offending nipple, was set to return to Britain for pre-film screenings at cinemas.

ANYTHING TO DECLARE?

Only two people signed the Declaration of Independence on 4 July 1776, John Hancock and Charles Thomson. Most of the other 56 (from the 13 existing states) signed on 2 August, although not all of the signers were present that day, and the last signature, that of Thomas McKean wasn't added until five years later. John Hancock, the President of the Congress and the first to sign, had so irked the British that, at the time of signing, the British government had put a price on his head. Perhaps this is why his signature on the Declaration is one of the most flamboyant of all. When signing he is reported to have said 'The British ministry can read that name without spectacles; let them double their reward.'

POLITICS IN WRITING

In all the practical work of our Party, all correct leadership is neces-
sarily 'from the masses, to the masses'. This means: take the ideas of
the masses (scattered and unsystematic ideas) and concentrate them
(through study turn them into concentrated and systematic ideas),
then go to the masses and propagate and explain these ideas until the
masses embrace them as their own, hold fast to them and translate
them into action, and test the correctness of these ideas in such action.
Then once again concentrate ideas from the masses and once again go
to the masses so that the ideas are persevered in and carried through.
And so on, over and over again in an endless spiral, with the ideas
becoming more correct, more vital and richer each time. Such is the
Marxist theory of knowledge.

Mao Tsetung, *The Little Red Book*

PRESIDENTIAL SCANDALS

In 1802, the notorious scaremon-
gering journalist James Callender
published a rumour that Thomas
Jefferson had secretly fathered
children by the slave Sally
Hemings. She was the illicit half-
sister of Jefferson's late wife
Martha and herself the daughter
of a female slave. The rumours
were not taken entirely seriously
until DNA testing in 1998 on
Jefferson's descendants showed
that it was very likely that Jefferson or one of his close male
relatives was the father of Eston,
Hemings' last son. A later study
by the Thomas Jefferson Founda-
tion concluded that it was indeed
likely that Eston came from presidential stock.

SPEAKERS OF THE HOUSE WHO
MET A STICKY END

Sir John Bussy: Speaker 1394–1398. *Beheaded 1399.*
William Tresham: Speaker 1439–1442, 1447, 1449–1450.
Murdered 1450.
Thomas Thorpe: Speaker 1453–1454. *Beheaded 1461.*
Sir John Wenlock: Speaker 1455–1456.
Killed at the Battle of Tewkesbury 1471.
Sir Thomas Tresham: Speaker 1459. *Beheaded 1471*
William Catesby: Speaker 1484. *Beheaded 1485.*
Sir Richard Empson: Speaker 1491-2. *Beheaded 1510.*
(On same day as Dudley)
Edmond Dudley: Speaker 1504. *Beheaded 1510.*
(On same day as Empson)
Sir Thomas More: Speaker 1523. *Beheaded 1535.*

Age of Margaret Thatcher when she stepped down from her role as 65
Prime Minister

TO PLAY THE PRESIDENT

Actors who have portrayed real US Presidents on film

Frank Austin (President Lincoln), *Court-Martial* (1928)

Sidney Blackmer (President Theodore Roosevelt), *This is My Affair* (1937)

Ed Beheler (President Jimmy Carter), *Sextette* (1978)

Robert V Barron (President Lincoln), *Bill & Ted's Excellent Adventure* (1989)

Ed Nelson (President Harry S Truman), *Brenda Starr* (1989)

Anthony Hopkins (President Nixon), *Nixon* (1995)

Rich Little (President Nixon's voice), *Bebe's Kids* (1992)

Pete Renady (President Lincoln's voice), *Bebe's Kids* (1992)

Bob Gill (President Kennedy), *Love Field* (1992)

Joe Alaskey (President Nixon), *Forrest Gump* (1994)

John William Galt (President Johnson), *Forrest Gump* (1994)

Jed Gillin (President Kennedy), *Forrest Gump* (1994)

Morris Ankrum (President Ulysses S Grant), *From the Earth to the Moon* (1958)

Ed Beheler (President Jimmy Carter), *The Last Boy Scout* (1991)

PRESIDENTIAL SCANDALS

'No one but the President seems to be expected... to look out for the general interests of the country' – Woodrow Wilson

US President Woodrow Wilson may have regarded himself as the representative of the people, but his personal life was not immune from scandal. In March 1915, he met a widow named Edith Bolling Galt. By May he had proposed, but the match was greeted with shock by some, as the president had himself lost his first wife, Ellen Louise Axson, only the previous August. Gossip flowed and there were even far-fetched rumours that Wilson had murdered his wife, or that he had been having an affair. Unbowed, Wilson and Galt were married in December.

QUOTE UNQUOTE

The right honourable gentleman is reminiscent of a poker. The only difference is that a poker gives off the occasional signs of warmth.
Benjamin Disraeli (on Robert Peel),
Prime Minister, 1868, 1874–1880

---

66 *Year in the 1900s when three British politicians were assaulted in Rhodesia (now Zimbabwe) on 12 January*

The broadcast was to be from Windsor Castle. [John] Reith chatted for a few minutes about Spain and other subjects; he had thought it right, he later explained, 'to behave as if nothing untoward or unusual was happening' – quite an undertaking in the circumstances. The signal was given and the former King began to speak. He declared his allegiance to the new monarch, and his sense of duty towards his country and the Empire, and then continued with the sentence which is the best remembered of anything he said in his whole life: 'You must believe me when I tell you that I have found it impossible to carry the heavy burden of responsibility and to discharge my duty as King as I would wish to do, without the help and support of the woman I love.' The decision to abdicate, he said, was his alone; he had taken it in the knowledge that his brother, 'with his long training in the public affairs of this country and with his fine qualities,' was well qualified to take his place: 'And he has one matchless blessing, enjoyed by so many of you and not bestowed on me – a happy home with his wife and children.' After that it only remained to pay due tribute to Queen Mary, Mr Baldwin and all others concerned and to embark on his peroration:

'I now quit altogether public affairs, and I lay down my burden. It may be some time before I return to my native land, but I shall always follow the fortunes of the British race and Empire with profound interest, and if at any time in the future I can be found of service to His Majesty in a private station I shall not fail.

'And now we all have a new King. I wish him, and you, his people, happiness and prosperity with all my heart. God bless you all. God Save the King.'

It was Edward VIII's speech, drafted with some help from Monckton and embellished but not substantially changed by Winston Churchill. He began nervously, noted Monckton, but gathered confidence, and ended almost with a shout. When it finished, he stood up, put an arm on Monckton's shoulder, and said: 'Walter, it is a far better thing I go to.'

Philip Ziegler, *King Edward VIII The Official Biography*

A POPULAR FIRST

The 1994 city council elections in Prague attracted the world's longest ever list of candidates on a ballot paper. There were 1,187 people fighting for influence in the capital in what was the Czech Republic's first municipal ballot. The second-longest ballot was for the 2003 election for governor of California. Eventual winner Arnold Schwarzenegger saw off the challenges of 134 other candidates.

The early days of MI5 were beset by low budgets.

QUOTE UNQUOTE

There are known knowns; there are things we know we know. We also know there are known unknowns; that is to say we know there are some things we do not know. But there are also unknown unknowns – the ones we don't know we don't know.
Donald Rumsfeld, US Secretary of Defence, 1975–1977, 2001–

BETTY'S IN CHARGE

When the House of Commons elected a woman as Speaker for the first time in its 700-year history in 1992, MPs broke with Commons protocol and stood and applauded Betty Boothroyd as she took her chair. Then the Labour MP for West Bromwich West, Boothroyd was the first Speaker since the war to be a member of the Opposition. She was also the first Speaker to have been a Tiller girl. Betty worked for the famous chorus line dancers before becoming an MP in 1974. When MPs asked what to call her when she became Deputy Speaker in 1992, she answered, 'Call me Madam.'

WOMEN IN PARLIAMENT

As of 1 March 2003, the following countries boasted the highest percentage of women in parliament in the world:

Country	Ratio of women to seats	Percentage of parliamentarians that are women
1. Rwanda	39/80	48.8
2. Sweden	158/349	45.3
3. Denmark	68/179	38
4. Finland	75/200	37.5
5. Netherlands	55/150	36.7
6. Norway	60/165	36.4
7= Cuba	219/609	36
7= Spain	126/350	36
9. Belgium	53/150	35.3
10. Costa Rica	20/57	35.1)

RULES OF THE HOUSE

What the Speaker of the House may and may not do...

The Speaker's seat is traditionally not contested at General Elections.

The Speaker must act in a completely impartial manner. He or she plays a role as a constituency MP but cannot raise constituents' issues in the Chamber.

The Speaker is elected at the start of each new Parliament. There are three deputies. The Speaker may exercise a casting vote in order to extend a debate or to maintain the status quo.

The Speaker must address members by their correct titles. As there are 658 names to learn, he or she must possess a capacious memory.

The Speaker presides over the House wearing a ceremonial black robe. A wig is optional.

The Speaker lives in the Speaker's House in the Palace of Westminster.

The Speaker represents the House of Commons in its dealings with the monarch.

MPs bow to the Speaker on leaving the House, and elsewhere in the Palace of Westminster (during the Speaker's procession, for instance). This is thought to derive from the time between 1550 and 1834, when the Commons occupied St Stephen's Chapel and members bowed to the altar, in front of which the Speaker sat.

IN OTHER WORDS

Some US political slang, old and new:

bloviate – to speak at length in a defiant, boastful way – first used to describe President Warren Harding and his friends

boodle – a bribe

boodler – someone who takes bribes

boondoggling – first used during Franklin Roosevelt's administration, to describe the 'make-work' projects that many thought wasteful

bulldozing – intimidating officials with threats of violence

carpetbagger – an unscrupulous politician who takes advantage of someone weaker or less fortunate

to crawfish – to backtrack from one's current position

lame duck – someone who has not been re-elected, but still has some of his or her term to serve

mugwump – a politician who won't follow the exact dictates of their party. Now known as being off-message.

roorback – a lie about a candidate that is circulated before the night of an election

to send up Salt River – to defeat the other candidate

THE UNION FLAG

Known correctly as the Union Flag, although more commonly as the Union Jack, the flag of the United Kingdom was designed to include the national emblem of each of its member countries. So the red cross of St George on the white background (for England), the diagonal red on white cross of St Patrick (for Ireland) and the diagonal white on blue cross of St Andrew (for Scotland) came together to form one of the most well-known of the world's flags. The Welsh dragon does not feature because in 1606 when James I created the flag, Wales had been united with England and was not considered a separate principality.

When and why the flag was christened 'Jack' is a contentious subject. It has been claimed that it serves as a tribute to its creator (James being Jacobus in Latin and Jacques in French), that it stems from Charles II's order that the flag should be flown only by ships of the Royal Navy as a 'jack' (a small flag at the ship's front) and even that it refers to the jackets worn by English or Scottish soldiers.

The current design was made official in 1801 as a royal flag and the order was given that it should be flown from all royal buildings and nowhere else. Now the flag is not only flown from certain government departments at the Queen's command, but also is often displayed at sporting events, during the last night of the Proms and on countless items of clothing and tourist souvenirs.

POLITICAL ANAGRAMS

Of which British Prime Minister is this an anagram
SAD THAT TONY BLAIR CHEERS HER ON
Answer on page 153.

A HISTORY OF THE HOUSE

Since the fifteenth century the House of Lords has been known as the Upper House and the House of Commons the Lower House. Back then membership of the House of Lords was made up of the Lords Spiritual (two Archbishops, 24 Diocesan Bishops) and the Lords Temporal, who were divided into three groups: hereditary peers, peers granted peerages by the sovereign on the advice of the Prime Minister, and the Law Lords, recruited from the ranks of Britain's High Court Judges.

The House of Lords is slightly smaller than the House of Commons and only seats 250 members. However, Barry and Pugin made the interior more impressive than the Commons and upholstered the seats in red leather. The chamber is dominated by an ornate royal throne where the sovereign sits during the opening of Parliament.

In 1909, the two Houses clashed when the Lords rejected a budget approved by the Commons. The result was the Parliamentary Act of 1911 under which the House of Lords lost its power of veto. The Parliamentary Act of 1949 further reduced the House of Lords' power to postpone bills.

In opposition Tony Blair said Labour was in favour of an elected second chamber.

After the 1997 election, Prime Minister Blair called for a fully appointed House of Lords. On 4 February 2003, the House of Lords voted for this measure (335 votes to 110) but it was defeated in the House of Commons (323 votes to 245), even though twenty-five members of the government, including four Cabinet ministers, voted against the proposal. In 1999, legislation finally abolished the right of hereditary peers to inherit a seat in the Lords along with their title.

A POPULAR LADY

On 18 July 1998, Graca Machel became the first woman to have been First Lady of two countries when she married the South African President, Nelson Mandela. Graca had previously been married to the president of neighbouring Mozambique, Samora Machel, until his death in 1986.

Initially the White House wasn't white at all but grey, the colour of the Virginia sandstone used to build it. Construction started in the early 1790s but when the Adams family moved in in 1800 (John Adams was the second president) the roof leaked and there was no running water.

The building was torched by the British in August 1814 but came back better and whiter. Smoke stains were painted over in white and it was duly christened the White House. But the only object known to have survived this period of change is a painting of George Washington, which now hangs in the East Room.

In the 1940s the whole building had to be reworked before it collapsed and President Truman temporarily moved across the road into Blair House at 1651 Pennsylvania Avenue.

Today's White House offers a tennis court, putting green, jogging track and billiard table. There is also a pool, a movie theatre and even a presidential bowling alley. President Nixon filled in the swimming pool to make room for more reporters, but as soon as Gerald Ford, a keen swimmer, replaced him he had another one dug.

America's first declaration of war was signed by James Madison in the Green Room. John Quincy Adams called it the Green Drawing Room because Thomas Jefferson used to cover the floor in a green canvas when he ate in there. The Red Room is the party room. During Madison's term the doors were opened every Wednesday for senators and congressmen to enjoy a snack and an informal chat. In the 1930s Eleanor Roosevelt gave press conferences in the Red Room for women reporters, as they were not allowed in her husband's press conferences. Visiting female dignitaries are put up in the Rose Room, and their male counterparts in the Lincoln Bedroom.

Press conferences, weddings and funerals have all been held in the East Room. Teddy Roosevelt's children even used it for roller-skating. Franklin Roosevelt kept his fishing mementos and an aquarium in there. John F Kennedy later put up a sailfish which he caught in Acapulco.

William Howard Taft was the 27th US President but the first to walk into the Oval Office, built in 1909. Taft positioned the office in the centre of the West Wing so that he would be more involved with the day-to-day operation of his presidency. But Franklin Roosevelt relocated it to the southeast corner in 1934. It was Theodore Roosevelt who ordered the construction of an extra west wing. At the time he had six children and things were getting a little crowded.

America...well knows that by once enlisting under other banners than her own, were they even the banners of foreign independence, she would involve herself beyond the power of extraction, in all the wars of interest and intrigue, of individual avarice, envy, and ambition, which assume the colours and usurp the standard of freedom. The fundamental maxims of her policy would insensibly change from liberty to force...She might become dictatress of the world. She would be no longer the ruler of her own spirit.

John Quincy Adams, address on 4 July 1821

THE RULES OF THE HOUSE

Although boisterous and rigorous debates are welcomed in parliament, they must always be tempered with acceptable language. Erskine May, who recorded parliamentary rules, wrote that, 'good temper and moderation are the characteristics of parliamentary language'. Insulting and abusive language, particularly when directed at other members, is not welcome. According to parliamentary record, insults such as blackguard, coward, git (a recent addition), guttersnipe, hooligan, rat, swine, stoolpigeon, behaving like a jackass, murderer, pharisee, cheeky young pup, impertinent puppy, nosey parker and traitor have all been objected to by Speakers over the years.

If such insults are voiced or hurled across the Chamber, the Speaker will ask for them to be withdrawn by the culprit. Rudeness can result in expulsion from the Chamber.

As well as keeping the language clean, members must also be careful not to call another member a liar, suggest that he has false motives or misrepresent his language.

The more ingenious can find ways to be insulting without being censured. Winston Churchill once used the phrase 'terminological inexactitude' to imply that a member was lying.

CHINESE PRIME MINISTERS AND COMMUNIST PARTY LEADERS

Prime Ministers		Communist Leaders	
1949–1976	Zhou Enlai	1935–1976	Mao Zedong
1976–1980	Hua Guofeng	1976–1981	Hua Guofeng
1980–1987	Zhao Ziyang	1981–1987	Hu Yaobang
1987–1998	Li Peng	1987–1989	Zhao Ziyang
1998–2003	Zhu Rongji	1989–2003	Jiang Zemin
2003–	Wen Jiabao	2003–	Hu Jintao

WHAT DO YOU MEAN, YOU WORK HERE?

A few years before he became Prime Minister, David Lloyd George went to Canada in 1899 and while he was there he shaved off his trademark moustache. When he returned to the House of Commons the speaker didn't recognise him.

QUOTE ON QUOTE

It is often said that the central lobby in the House of Commons is the third easiest place in Europe to pick people up after Funland in Leicester Square and the arrival lounge at Rome airport.
Alan Clark, Conservative MP

MARRIED AT HOME

Grover Cleveland was the first President to be married on the White House grounds. At the age of 49, he wed 21-year-old Frances Folsom in the Blue Room on 2 June 1886. His new wife was the daughter of a good friend of his, so he had known her since she was a baby. He had even bought her a baby carriage. Their daughter, Esther Cleveland, subsequently became the only child of a President to have been born in the White House.

HOW TO LOSE YOUR HEAD

Pope John Paul II named Thomas More the patron saint of politicians in 2000. More was not a man afraid to stand up for his principles. On 6 July 1535 he was beheaded for refusing to swear the Act of Succession or the Oath of Supremacy.

Born in Milk Street, London, on 7 February 1478, More practiced as a barrister, lived in a monastery and translated Lucian into Latin with his friend Erasmus and entered parliament in 1504, championing the poor and courting controversy. He briefly bowed out of politics after angering Henry VII and made his comeback only after the king's death.

More was initially popular with Henry VIII. As Speaker of the House of Commons, he helped to establish the parliamentary privilege of free speech. He also became the first layman to be appointed Lord Chancellor. But he clashed with the king first over his plans to divorce Catherine of Aragon and then over Henry's renunciation of Catholicism. More's last words on the scaffold were: 'The King's good servant, but God's First.'

CURRENT MEMBERS OF THE NORTH ATLANTIC TREATY ORGANISATION (NATO)

Belgium	1949	Lithuania	2004
Bulgaria	2004	Luxembourg	1949
Canada	1949	Netherlands	1949
Czech Rep	1999	Norway	1949
Denmark	1949	Poland	1999
Estonia	2004	Portugal	1949
France	1949	Romania	2004
Germany	1965	Slovakia	2004
Greece	1952	Slovenia	2004
Hungary	1999	Spain	1982
Iceland	1949	Turkey	1952
Italy	1949	United Kingdom	1949
Latvia	2004	United States	1949

President Bush welcomed the new members of 2004 in what was the largest Nato expansion since 1949. 'As witness to some of the great crimes of the last century, our new members bring moral clarity to the purposes of our alliance... they are stepping forward to secure the lives and freedoms of others,' he said.

SHAKESPEARE ON POLITICS

Political rivalries make or break careers. Shakespeare's Antony died in the shadow of Octavius, later Augustus, the first emperor of Rome. At least he was warned...

ANTONY
Say to me
Whose fortunes shall rise higher: Caesar's or mine?

SOOTHSAYER
Caesar's. Therefore, O Antony, stay not by his side.
Thy daemon, that thy spirit which keeps thee, is
Noble, courageous, high, unmatchable,
Where Caesar's is not. But near him thy angel
Becomes afeard, as being o'erpowered. Therefore
Make space enough between you.

...If thou dost play with him at any game
Thou art sure to lose; and, of that natural luck
He beats thee 'gainst the odds. Thy lustre thickens
When he shines by. I say again, thy spirit
Is all afraid to govern thee near him;
But he away, 'tis noble.

Anthony and Cleopatra, Act II, Scene iii

When Presidents – and their wives – pen their memoirs, the reviews are not always kind...

Jimmy Carter, *Keeping Faith*
The feeling is often that of a man doing his duty, performing a chore, rather than a labor of love or even enjoyment. Carter grubs with painful diligence. No one will dispute authorship. This is clearly his very own work... No experienced non-fiction editor appears to have laid a glove on it. James Bell, *The Boston Globe*

Bill Clinton, *My Life*
The book itself can only be described as bizarre. It isn't just that it's badly written, as so many political memoirs are, or that the sections on Hillary and Monica are weirdly abrupt and uninformative, particularly in contrast to how carefully and lovingly crafted is Clinton's story about the time his stepfather shot a pistol at his mother. But since there aren't many gory details of the Lewinsky saga that we didn't already know, one probably shouldn't blame the former president for breezing rapidly through the whole sordid episode. Anne Applebaum, *The Daily Telegraph*

Hillary Clinton, *Living History*
It is sad how little of this fiery, opinionated creature gets into her memoirs. Hillary's idea of a great anecdote is when she bumps into the Prime Minister of Norway and – wait for it – Mrs Brundtland has read Mrs Clinton's health plan and wants to discuss it! It's probably the way she tells them. Allison Pearson, *The Daily Telegraph*

Lyndon Johnson, *The Vantage Point*
When he saw his words on paper, he said, 'Goddammit! Get that vulgar language of mine out of there. What do you think this is, the tale of an uneducated cowboy? It's a presidential memoir, damn it, and I've got to come out looking like a statesman, not some backwoods politician.' ...The result, published in 1971, was so leaden that much of it read like a parody of a presidential memoir. Michael Beschloss, *Texas Monthly*

Richard Nixon, *RN*
The book's main importance lies in its potential usefulness to Nixon revisionists who will seek to restore him to the place that he feels he should adorn, the pantheon of great Presidents. Out of this bible – big and fat and imposing, like all holy scriptures – chapter and verse will be cited and adversaries denounced. James MacGregor Burns, *The New York Times Book Review*

Ronald Reagan, *An American Life*
During his quarter-century in public service Ronald Reagan was many things... but he was never, ever, dull. Still, all things must come to all men, so now in the years of his retirement dullness has visited itself upon Ronald Wilson Reagan and caused him to commit [to paper] *An American Life*... a thoroughly soporific and mostly useless book. Jonathan Yardley, *The Washington Post*

Year in the 1800s that American General Custer made his last stand against the Natives at Little Bighorn. All of his soldiers were killed

POLITICS IN PICTURES

The labour party

QUOTE UNQUOTE

As I was saying when I was so rudely interrupted 14 years ago...
Ken Livingstone, former leader of the Greater
London Council, which was abolished in 1986,
on being elected Mayor of London in 2000

WAITING TO PROTEST

Four African-American students, Franklin McCain, Joseph McNeil,
Ezell Blair Jr and David Richmond, sat down at a 'whites-only'
Woolworth lunch counter in Greensboro, North Carolina, USA, on
1 February 1960 and did not get up again until 25 July 1960. The
peaceful sit-in is the longest in history.

POLITICS IN WRITING

Whereas Charles Stuart, King of England, is and standeth convicted,
attained and condemned of High Treason and other high crimes; and
sentence upon Saturday last was pronounced against him by this
court, to be put to death by the severing of his head from his body; of
which sentence execution yet remaineth to be done: These are therefore to will and require you to see the said Sentence executed, in the
open street before Whitehall, upon the morrow, being the thirtieth
day of this instant month of January, between the hours of ten in the
morning and five in the afternoon, with full effect. And for so doing,
this shall be your warrant.

Charles I's death warrant

*Number of Nazi party members killed by Hitler when voted into power in 77
June 1934 because he questioned their loyalty*

Megalomaniac Romanian President Nicolae Ceausescu succumbed to delusions of grandeur when he built The Victory of Socialism Centre, a vast palace from which he wished to rule his long-suffering country. The building is the second largest in the world. Designed by 700 Romanian architects, the shrine to the Communist ruler stands at 84 metres high and is 330,000 square metres. It took 20,000 Romanian workers five years to construct. One sixth of Bucharest was flattened to make way for the monster HQ, which was intended to house the President, Parliament and government. Complete with anti-atomic underground layers, it wasn't cheap – 30% of national finances were ploughed into the project.

The building contains around 3,000 exquisite rooms, each an overwhelming display of polished marble, silk curtains, gilded aluminium, carved wood panels and hand-woven silk tapestries. Every material used is Romanian. There is a 1,000-square-metre carpet weighing 14 tonnes, which needed special machines to make it. Inlaid floor and carpet designs mirror the decorated ceilings. The chandeliers were carved from 3,500 tons of crystal. The largest chandelier has 7,000 and weighs three tonnes.

However, Ceausescu himself was finished before his dream home was. A revolutionary mob surrounded the palace on 22 December 1989, and the President and his wife Elena attempted to escape by helicopter via a retractable roof on the Unification Hall. They weren't quite fast enough, and were caught and executed three days later by firing squad. The Romanian people were uncomfortable with the legacy of the palace, but blowing the thing up would have been expensive. Instead, the giant structure was renamed the Palace of Parliament and serves to house the new democratic parliament, a change of fortunes that should have its creator spinning in his grave.

POLITICS IN POETRY

There is nothing so bad or so good that you will not find
Englishmen doing it; but you will never find an
Englishmen in the wrong. He does everything on
Principle. He fights you on patriotic principles; he robs
You on business principles; he enslaves you on imperial
Principles; he bullies you on manly principles; he
Supports his king on loyal principles and cuts off his
King's head on republican principles.
George Bernard Shaw, *The Man of Destiny* (1898)

THE CURSE OF TECUMSEH

Between 1840 and 1960 every President elected in the 20-year cycle – in a year ending in '0' – died while in office. This misfortune is attributed to 'The Curse of Tecumseh', named after a Shawnee Indian chief whose brother predicted this presidential misery in 1836.

William Henry Harrison, elected in 1840 : died of pneumonia on 4 April, 1841 after giving a particularly long inaugural speech in the snow with no coat on.

Abraham Lincoln, elected in 1860: shot by John Wilkes Booth on 14 April 1865 and died the following day.

James Garfield, elected in 1880: shot by Charles Guiteau on 2 July 1881 at a railway station, dying two months later on 19 September.

William McKinley, re-elected in 1900: shot in Buffalo, New York by Leon Czolgosz, an unemployed Socialist, on 6 September 1901. Died a week later.

Warren Harding, elected in 1920: died of a heart attack on 2 August 1923. He had caught pneumonia after becoming the first president to visit Alaska in the same year.

Franklin Roosevelt, re-elected in 1940: after leading his country through the Great Depression and World War Two, he suffered a cerebral haemorrhage while on holiday in Warm Springs, Georgia, on 12 April 1945.

John F Kennedy, elected in 1960: shot on 22 November 1963.

Ronald Reagan, who was elected in 1980: survived an assassination attempt in 1981, and was the first to break the curse. George W Bush, elected in 2000, will be hoping that Reagan was not the exception to the rule. It is worth noting that both survived a threat to their lives; Reagan from a gunman, and Bush from a pretzel.

THE LIVING DEAD

When Ernesto Alvear tried to vote in the Chilean general election of 1999, ballot officials in his home town of Valparaiso claimed that he had been dead for 10 years. It was the third time Alvear had been turned away from polling stations because officials thought he was dead, despite appearing in person to cast his vote: 'I'm tired of complaining without any success. I think this is the last time I am going to bother,' lamented the 74-year-old. It was eventually discovered that a man with the same name had died in the same town some years earlier, thus causing the mix-up, and Alvear was allowed to cast his vote.

Youngest
William Pitt, 'The Younger', was 24 when he took office. He went to Pembroke College, Cambridge, in 1773 at the age of 14 and graduated three years later.

Oldest
Viscount Palmerston was over 70 when he took office in 1855.
William Gladstone served as Prime Minister until he was 84.

Longest lived
Macmillan lived the longest of any Prime Minister to date – he was 92 years and 322 days when he died in 1986.

Oldest to marry
The oldest Prime Minister to marry was David Lloyd George, who tied the knot at 80 years and 279 days.

Heaviest
The Marquess of Salisbury, who was elected Prime Minister in 1885, was so overweight that he had a special sunken bath built, so that he could get in and out more easily.

Most siblings
Sir Robert Walpole was one of 17 children. He went on to have six of his own.

Most children
Earl Grey had 17 children, the most born to any Prime Minister. His first son became Secretary of State for War.

Most distant birthplace
Andrew Bonar Law is the only Prime Minister to have been born outside the British Isles. He was born in Kingston, Canada, over 3,000 miles from London.

Longest neck
The Earl of Liverpool, Prime Minister at the end of the Napoleonic wars, was said to have the longest neck in England.

First to have television in 10 Downing Street
John Logie Baird gave Ramsey MacDonald a private demonstration of the television at Number 10 in 1930.

First to have television in Westminster
Harold Wilson requested a colour television in his office at Westminster in 1968, although he did first have to persuade MI5 that it wouldn't be a security risk. He later swapped it for a black and white model when the bill proved too expensive.

QUOTE UNQUOTE

I've often thought that the process of ageing could be slowed down if it had to go through Congress.
George Bush, US President 1989–1993

POLITICAL ANAGRAMS

Of which MP is this an anagram
I'M TORY PLAN B
Answer on page 153.

20TH CENTURY UK PRIME MINISTERS

Tony Blair 1997	*(Labour)*
John Major 1990–1997	*(Conservative)*
Margaret Thatcher 1979–1990	*(Conservative)*
James Callaghan 1976–1979	*(Labour)*
Edward Heath 1970-1974	*(Conservative)*
Harold Wilson 1964–1970;1974–1976	*(Labour)*
Alec Douglas-Home 1963–1964	*(Conservative)*
Harold Macmillan 1957–1963	*(Conservative)*
Anthony Eden 1955–1957	*(Conservative)*
Clement Attlee 1945–1951	*(Labour)*
Winston Churchill 1940–1945, 1951–1955	*(Conservative)*
Neville Chamberlain 1937–1940	*(Conservative)*
Ramsay MacDonald 1924, 1929–1935	*(Labour)*
Stanley Baldwin 1923; 1924–1929, 1935–1937	*(Conservative)*
Andrew Bonar Law 1922–1923	*(Conservative)*
David Lloyd George 1916–1922	*(Liberal)*
HH Asquith 1908–1916	*(Liberal)*
Henry Campbell-Bannerman 1905–1908	*(Liberal)*
Arthur James Balfour 1902–1905	*(Conservative)*

THE RULES OF THE HOUSE

Eating in the chamber of the House of Commons is forbidden. Apart from discreet sips of water, drinking is also not allowed. There is one exception to this rule. The Chancellor, on his big day – Budget Day – may enjoy an alcoholic drink. While delivering the Budget Speech the Chancellor is allowed to fortify himself with the liquid refreshment of his choice. Disraeli is thought to have favoured brandy and water, while Gladstone apparently consumed sherry and beaten egg from his pomatum pot. The diarist Henry Lucy described the liquid in the pot as resembling 'a preparation for the hair as it might look in sultry weather'. Derek Heathcote Amory reportedly took a concoction of milk, honey and rum. More recently Kenneth Clarke was partial to neat whisky. After his Budget statement in July 1997, Gordon Brown was congratulated by the Leader of the Opposition, William Hague, 'on his fortitude in delivering his speech with only the assistance of water.'

Age in years of the oldest person to be electronically tagged by a British court 81

World leaders and their country retreats

Camp David

President Franklin Roosevelt's sinuses were sensitive to the muggy heat of Washington DC and he liked getting some fresh air on the presidential yacht US Potomac. When this practice was jeopardised during the Second World War, an alternative retreat had to be found. So in 1942 a site 1,800 feet above sea level in the Catoctin Mountains in Maryland, just 70 miles from the capital, was groomed as a presidential hideaway. Over $20,000 was spent on constructing the main lodge. Roosevelt named his new retreat 'Shangri-La' after the mountain kingdom in James Hilton's *Lost Horizon*. It was renamed Camp David by President Eisenhower in 1953 in honour of his grandson.

Camp David is operated by Navy personnel. Troops from Marine Barracks in Washington provide security. The president flies the half-hour helicopter ride from the capital in Marine One. Winston Churchill discussed plans for the Allies' invasion of Europe with Eisenhower there, Khrushchev visited Eisenhower, Lyndon Johnson held Vietnam War discussions and President Jimmy Carter chose the retreat for the meeting between Middle East leaders which led to the Camp David Accords in 1978.

There is a pool, a putting green and a driving range at Camp David along with tennis courts, a gymnasium and numerous guest cabins all named after types of tree. The presidential cabin is called Aspen Lodge.

Konstantin Palace

In 2003 President Putin opened a new state residence in the eighteenth-century Italianate Konstantin Palace, a former Tsarist residence, just outside St Petersburg. The building had been transformed into a government residence to host international conferences and summits following a $300 million restoration, which had restored the palace's lavish gilt and frescoed halls to their eighteenth-century magnificence. The project was completed just in time for St Petersburg's 300th anniversary.

Konstantin Palace was the brainchild of Peter the Great who founded St Petersburg in May 1703. Built between 1720 and 1750 on a hill overlooking the Gulf of Finland and named after the son of Emperor Paul I, the palace is decorated with great crystal chandeliers, friezes and gilded paintings embellishing columned walls and arched ceilings. The palace was on the front line between German and Soviet troops during the Second World War and was seriously damaged.

Between 2001 and 2003, the palace underwent a $300 million renovation in preparation for St Petersburg's 300th birthday party. Close to 6,000 workers worked round the clock and in the last days soldiers assisted in the clearing up. Luxurious villas named after Russian cities were constructed on the palace grounds to house visiting world leaders.

Chequers

Chequers gets its name from its first owner, who was the Chancellor of the Exchequer. Rebuilt in the Tudor period, it was bought and renovated in 1909 by Lord Lee of Fareham, who donated it to the nation in 1917 so that the Prime Minister of the day would have a country estate to retreat to. The gift was approved by Parliament in the Chequers Estate Act 1917. There was also a maintenance grant to go with it, 'for the official occupant to live in a fashion deliberately designed to encourage regular weekend visits'. Three years later Lee also added over 1,000 acres to complete the package. The Buckinghamshire house is endowed with an impressive collection of paintings and Oliver Cromwell's death mask, as well as Lord Nelson's watch and a ring belonging to Elizabeth I. Winston Churchill made many of his addresses to the nation from Chequers, including the rousing 'we shall fight them on the beaches' speech. In 1973, Edward Heath added a swimming-pool to the grounds, paid for by American Ambassador Walter Annenberg in return for hospitality shown to Richard Nixon on his visits there.

Château Rambouillet

The Château de Rambouillet is in the town of Rambouillet, a handy 50 kilometres south-west of Paris. Starting out as a simple manor house in the fourteenth century, it was later expanded into the Renaissance-style château it is now. It was bought by the Crown during the reign of Louis XVI, before being leased to the Duc de la Tremoille. In 1896 President Felix Faure took a holiday there, and since then it has been used by presidents to entertain and give hunting parties for foreign dignitaries, royalty and heads of state. In November 1975 President Valéry Giscard D'Estaing organised the first G7 summit at the château, and the Kosovo peace talks were held here in 1990.

Villa Certosa

There is no national retreat for the Italian leader, but billionaire leader Silvio Berlusconi has done his best to convert one of his seven residences into a Camp David equivalent. The Villa Certosa is a luxury residence on the island of Sardinia. The 2,500 square-metre house is surrounded by 50 hectares of park on the northern Emerald coast. There is a private beach, fitness centre, tennis court and private cinema as well as an artificial lake. Berlusconi planted a 500-year-old carob tree close by, which he picked up at the botanic gardens in Cagliari, the Sardinian capital. Various heads of state have been entertained on the island, including President Putin. The Russian was accompanied by three warships, which were parked neatly in the Villa's bay. Berlusconi even hired the tenor Andrea Bocelli for a private concert in Putin's honour.

QUOTE UNQUOTE

*Nowhere is there a man who has so much power
and so little to show for it.*
William Gladstone,
Prime Minister 1868–1874, 1880–1885, 1886 and 1892–1894

ASSASSINATION ATTEMPTS

In 1950 Puerto Rican nationalists attempted to assassinate Harry Truman in his sleep. Griselio Torresola and Oscar Collazo were members of the Puerto Rican Nationalist Party whose leader, Harvard graduate Pedro Albizu Campos, had been the victim of racism in the American army during World War One. He was bitter about his experience and wanted independence for Puerto Rico. Torresola and Collazo bought one way tickets to Washington and said goodbye to their families. Unusually, the president was based at Blair House, further along Presidential Avenue, as the White House was being renovated, which was less well-protected than the White House.

On 1 November Torresola taught his accomplice how to handle his gun at their hotel before the pair took a taxi to Blair House. They were armed with 69 rounds of ammunition. At around 2pm, the nationalists attacked from opposite side of the building. They killed one of the seven guards on duty and wounded two others before Torresola was himself killed and Collazo wounded. The heroic efforts of one guard, Private Coffelt, helped to prevent Torresola reaching the President. He was taken by surprise by the gunman and mortally wounded, managed to shoot him dead before losing consciousness. Truman commuted Collazo's death sentence to life imprisonment and went on to serve the rest of his presidential term. Collazo was eventually released in 1979 on the orders of President Jimmy Carter.

POLITICS IN WRITING

The days and weeks of screwed-up smiles and laboured courtesy, the mock geniality, the hearty shake of the filthy hand, the chuckling reply that must be made to the coarse joke, the loathsome, choking compliment that must be paid to the grimy wife and sluttish daughter, the indispensable flattery of the vilest religious prejudices, the wholesale deglutition of hypocritical pledge.

Lord Salisbury, Prime Minister 1885–1886, 1886–1892,
1895–1902, describing the joys of electioneering from
Neil Hamilton's *Politics' Strangest Characters*

If it has fallen to my destiny to start a fight to cut out the cancer of bent and twisted journalism in our country with the simple sword of truth and the trusty shield of British fair play, so be it. I am ready for the fight.

With these words, former Cabinet Minister Jonathan Aitken made his stand for truth during his libel action against the *Guardian* newspaper and Granada Television in 1997. By the end of the whole sorry affair, he would be remembered in history for eating more humble pie than any MP in political history. Aitken was fighting to clear his name following allegations that he allowed an Arab friend to pay his bill for a stay at the Ritz Hotel in Paris. Aitken had accepted that such a payment would have contravened the government's code of conduct and resigned from John Major's government in 1995.

During the trial Aitken asked his teenage daughter, Victoria, to lie for him. Before she could, however, a *Guardian* investigative reporter produced evidence that led to the collapse of Aitken's case.

Aitken had already lost his Thanet South seat in the 1997 General Election, but now his wife Lolicia left him and he declared himself bankrupt. He owed the *Guardian* and Granada Television about £2 million in legal costs. Debt collectors seized possessions from his Westminster home. In 1998 he was sentenced to 18 months in prison for perjury and perverting the course of justice, as the judge labelled Aitken's story a 'web of deceit'. In June 1999 he began his sentence at Belmarsh jail near Woolwich, south London. 'I was terrified and felt utterly hopeless,' he recalls in his book, *Psalms for People Under Pressure*.

Aitken has since admitted his 'eternal shame' for asking his daughter to lie. He revealed how his guilty conscience had led him to plunge 'deep into the waters of Christianity', and blamed pride, 'the deadliest of sins', for his deceit. 'The political graveyards are littered with the long-forgotten corpses of ex-future prime ministers, so any such label should have made a wise man humble,' he said. 'In fact... I took myself far too seriously.'

LORD OF THE JUNGLE

During a debate on the Labour government's Aircraft and Shipbuilding Industries Bill in 1976, former Tory minister Michael Heseltine broke with Commons protocol by seizing the Speaker's Mace and brandishing it at his Labour colleagues as they celebrated winning the vote. The sight of the MP behaving in such an unbridled fashion promptly earned him the nickname 'Tarzan'.

It was South Africa's fourth Prime Minister, Daniel François Malan (1948–1954) who established the first exclusively Afrikaner government. He began the policy of racial segregation that became known as apartheid, which in Afrikaans means 'apartness'. Malan was ordained as a clergyman of the Dutch Reformed Church in 1905 and travelled South Africa and the Belgian Congo (now the Democratic Republic of Congo) and Rhodesia (now Zimbabwe) as a preacher. He joined JMB Hertzog's new National Party in 1915 and became the first editor of *Die Burger*, the party's newspaper, before becoming Minister for the Interior, Education and Public Health in 1924.

Malan was instrumental in the creation of the Gesuiwerde Party (a 'Purified' National Party) that was formed in 1934 when he and 19 fellow MPs broke away from the newly formed coalition government of Hertzog and Jan Christiaan Smuts. The GNP later became the Herenigde National Party (the Reunited National Party or Volksparty) and took power in 1948 with Malan as Prime Minister after their support for Germany in the Second World War boosted the nationalist cause. While Smuts' Union Party had supported Britain, Malan's campaign was based on white supremacy, racial segregation and the control of migrant black workers. One by one, barriers to racial integration were erected in the form of acts such as the Prohibition of Mixed Marriages Act 1949, the Population Registration Act 1950, the Native Laws Amendment Act 1952 and the Reservation of Separate Amenities Act 1953. Malan retired in 1954 once he had succeeded in separating nearly all aspects of South African life according to colour. He died in 1959.

QUOTE UNQUOTE

A body of five hundred men chosen at random from amongst the unemployed.
David Lloyd-George, British Prime Minister 1916–1922

SIGN HERE, PLEASE

There are petitions and then there are petitions. By the end of their collection, Jubilee 2000, which campaigned for the cancellation of Third World debt, had collected a record 24,319,181 signatures from 160 countries. The organisation, now known as Jubilee Research, continues to campaign for the cancellation of unpayable debts from the world's poorest countries.

PUPPET STATE

On 21 July 2000, auction house Sotheby's concluded its sale of 'Spitting Image' puppets, put up for auction by their creator, Roger Law. An online sale followed a live auction at Sotheby's the previous week, which raised a substantial sum of money some of which went to help restore the Hackney Empire theatre in east London.

Number of lots: **301**
Total sales: **£370,105**

Top sellers:

Margaret Thatcher ('patronising' version)	£11,224	(39 bids)
Mick Jagger	£7,545	
Ronald and Nancy Reagan	£6,494	(57 bids)
Sir John Gielgud	£5,400	
Margaret Thatcher ('angry' version)	£5,299	(37 bids)
Norman Tebbit (in leather)	£4,858	(32 bids)
The Duke of Edinburgh	£4,496	(46 bids)
George Best	£4,490	
Margaret Thatcher with Dennis	£4,490	(47 bids)
The Queen	£4,383	(32 bids)
Elvis	£4,162	(41 bids)
Peter O'Toole	£4,122	
Prince of Wales	£3,496	(36 bids)
John Major with Norma	£3,165	
Tony and Cherie	£3,128	
Laurence Olivier	£3,095	(54 bids)
Ross Perot	£2,981	
Sid James	£2,098	

The many celebrities who attended included Lord Owen, Michael Winner, Gary Rhodes, Ian Hislop and Sir Paddy Ashdown, some of whom watched themselves be sold off. Former Deputy Prime Minister Michael Heseltine praised the show for boosting his profile. 'I was an obscure member of the British Government, a common or garden Cabinet minister – and suddenly wherever I went, Hezza or Michael. I was a celebrity.'

FREE-THINKING

The London-based society Anti-Slavery is the oldest international human rights organisation in the world. It was founded in 1839 when it was known as the British and Foreign Anti-Slavery Society. Today its primary function is to lobby governments to make the abolition of slavery a more urgent priority.

Ambition. Politicians can't live with it, can't live without it, as the Bard often noted.

CARDINAL WOLSEY
Cromwell, I charge thee, fling away ambition:
By that sin fell the angels. How can man then,
The image of his maker, hope to win by it?
Love thyself last; cherish those hearts that hate thee;
Corruption wins not more than honesty.

Henry VIII, Act III Scene ii

PEER PRESSURE

The members of the House of Lords, in order of rank:

Prince (of the Blood Royal)
Archbishop • Duke
Marquess
Earl and Countess
Viscount • Baron

THE RICH AND THE NOT SO RICH

US Presidents and their money

George Washington (Federalist)
1789 to 1797
Born into money, Washington went on to marry wealthy widow Martha Dandridge Custis and used the vast resources he had acquired to lead the American Revolution. His estate was valued at more than $500,000 and his plantation at Mount Vernon housed 300 slaves, half of whom were his own.

Andrew Jackson (Democrat)
1829 to 1837
Raised by a prosperous uncle, Jackson practised as a lawyer and made a fortune from real estate. He twice married Rachel Donelson, a wealthy divorcee (once before her divorce was confirmed and again afterwards), and he owned a race track and he indulged in gambling with considerable success. As General he profited from negotiating land from Native Americans.

Theodore 'Teddy' Roosevelt (Republican) *1901 to 1909*
His grandfather was one of the richest bankers and merchants in New York City, but Roosevelt lost money in a ranching venture in the Dakota Territories and after his presidency had to support himself through his writing.

*As the first female arrived in their midst, the
MPs clamoured to be chosen to give her the tour of
the De-robing room.*

POLITICAL ANAGRAMS

Of which British Prime Minister could the following be said?
WE WANT A MILD LEGISLATOR
Answer on page 153.

POLITICS IN POETRY

Now would I not on politics enthuse?
For men apon their word cannot be true,
But, rant and rave 'pon what they mighten do,
If granted vote from public; well misled.
For weeks till 'lection come they'll rant and rave,
But by ignoring it, I'll better be.
My ear becometh weary of it all,
When of diverse reasons politicians seem to be.
And ne'er follow the same ideals as me.

Daphne Grant, *Politics*

Thursday 16 July

I suppose today was the high point of my social life to date – in so far as that depends upon my status as a politician. As I boasted to Charles Howard, 'I have got the Queen at four, the Prime Minister at six, and a private dinner with the American Ambassador at eight...' 'Watch out it is not God at midnight,' he answered, quite wittily.

It was my first time at Buck House garden, although to get to it we walked through that courtyard where I remember dismounting for the great Armstrong-Jones wedding ball in 1959, when Dukey tried to pick up Jane. Vast numbers of people, most of them in all-fitting and low quality morning dress, with stained and dog-eared grey toppers. The garden is rather featureless, although the beds and borders are most densely planted and the edges crazily clipped. The south side of the Palace is undistinguished in yellow sandstone and a bit of a muddle, rather like the northern aspect of Ston Easton. The tea was delicious, a sort of Indian Hukwa, and so was the fruit cake. Other items, like the drop scones and most of the patisserie were less good...

When you see the Queen in the flesh she is always smaller and more beautifully made up than one remembers. She was wearing a white silk coat (like Jane) and a navy blue straw hat. We had to leave early as I had been warned that there might be trouble at the '22 Committee concerning the press releases from the Home affairs meetings which Willie [Whitelaw] had addresses. But in fact nothing was raised and we went on to Downing Street, arriving with the first guests.

Alan Clark Diaries, *Into Politics*

IT'S A SCANDAL

On Christmas Eve 1974, the Australian police finally caught up with the fugitive John Stonehouse. Stonehouse, formerly a Labour MP for Walsall, had served as Postmaster General under Harold Wilson but fled earlier in 1974 when the Department of Trade and Industry looked into his affairs (having not been appointed to the shadow cabinet he had set up fraudulent businesses as a source of income). He faked his death and left behind a wife, a daughter and huge debts. His only trace was a pile of clothes lying on a Miami beach. Six months after his arrest in Australia he was deported to the UK where he was sentenced to seven years' imprisonment on 18 counts of theft, fraud and deception. He was released in 1979.

Stonehouse's former secretary and mistress Sheila Buckley had been with him when he was arrested and the couple married in 1981. Back in Australia, the police were reportedly miffed at discovering that Stonehouse was not in fact Lord Lucan, who was wanted in England for murder.

'So this is the working class, eh?
Is the model actual size?'

OLDEST SERVING BRITISH PRIME MINISTERS

	Age at end of term
1. William E. Gladstone (Liberal) 1809–1894	**84**
2= Viscount Palmerston (Liberal) 1784–1865	**80**
2= Winston S Churchill (Conservative) 1874–1955	**80**
4. Benjamin Disraeli (Conservative) 1804–1880	**75**
5. Earl Russell (Liberal) 1792–1866	**73**
6. Marquess of Salisbury (Conservative) 1830–1902	**72**
7= Duke of Portland (Coalition) 1738–1809	**71**
7= Sir H. Campbell-Bannerman (Liberal) 1836–1908	**71**
7= Neville Chamberlain (Coalition) 1869–1940	**71**
10. Earl of Wilmington (Whig) 1673–1743	**70**

MASONIC HISTORY

The Freemasons are perhaps the best known secret political society. But they are not the oldest Masonic lodge. The written records of Aitchison's Haven, a Masonic lodge in Musselburgh, Scotland, date back to 9 January 1599. It shut down in 1856. Mary's Chapel lodge in Edinburgh is the oldest Masonic lodge still in existence, and can be traced back to 31 July 1599.

FIRST PRIME MINISTERS

The first 10 men to be Prime Minister

Name	Party	Date of office	Constituencies
Sir Robert Walpole (1676–1745)	Whig	1721–1742	Castle Rising & King's Lynn
Sir Spencer Compton (1673-1743)	Whig	1742–1743	Rye, E. Grinstead & Sussex
Henry Pelham (1696–1754)	Whig	1743–1754	Seaford & Sussex
Thomas Pelham-Holles (1693–1768)	Whig	1754–1756, 1757–1762	House of Lords
William Cavendish (1720–1764)	Whig	1756–1757	Derbyshire
John Stuart (1713–1792)	Tory	1762–1763	House of Lords
George Grenville (1712–1770)	Whig	1763–1765	Buckingham
Charles Watson Wentworth (1730–82)	Whig	1765–1766	House of Lords
Augustus Henry Fitzroy (1735–1811)	Whig	1766–1770	Bury St Edmunds
Lord Frederick North (1732–1792)	Tory	1770–1782	Banbury

INSIDE CENTRAL GOVERNMENT

Whips are the parliamentary bad boys. When MPs take on this post, they become the school prefects of the House of Commons and are expected to keep their colleagues in line. In particular it is their job to ensure that MPs don't vote against the party line, and they have a range of incentives and deterrents at their disposal to pressure their fellow MPs into staying 'on message', not all of which could be said to be above board. 'The Whip' is also the name given to the document that details the next week's business, which each MP receives. On it, the importance of any voting items is demonstrated by the number of times the item is underlined – once, twice or three times. Parties expect their MPs to turn up and vote with the party on three-line whips, and it is considered a serious offence if they fail to do so. An MP or Peer who fails to attend a three-line whip may have the Whip withdrawn, which effectively expels him or her from the Parliamentary party, unless the Whip is later restored, which it generally is after a suitably chastening length of time. To stave off Parliament fatigue when there are a lot of items to vote on, MPs can pair with an Opposition MP. By agreeing not to attend a vote, the pair cancel out each other's votes without undermining the voting strength of their parties.

FIGHTING FOR THE RIGHT TO BE EQUAL

In 1897 Millicent Fawcett founded the National Union of Women's Suffrage and began a campaign to win women the vote. But Fawcett's peaceful movement failed to win over the majority of MPs. Frustrated by the lack of progress, Emmeline Pankhurst and her daughters Christabel and Sylvia set up the Women's Social and Political Union in 1903. The Union became known as the Suffragettes. They were prepared to resort to violence. 'Deeds, not words' was their motto.

In May 1905, a deputation of women appealed to the Prime Minister and were told to be patient. However, they chose to take action and began a campaign during which they interrupted political meetings, set fire to churches (the Church of England was unsympathetic to their cause) and smashed windows in Oxford Street. They chained themselves to the Buckingham Palace railings, went on hunger strike and hired boats on which they sailed up the Thames shouting abuse at Parliament. Politicians were attacked on their way to work and their homes were fire bombed. Some suffragettes also refused to pay their tax.

When war came, Pankhurst called off the campaign of violence and women played a vital role in the war effort. It didn't go unnoticed. The Women's Suffrage Bill was debated in the House of Commons in June 1917. In 1918, the Representation of the People Act gave the vote to women, but not to all women. Those over the age of 30 could vote providing they were householders, the wives of householders, occupied a property with an annual rent of £5 or were university graduates. Women did not achieve full voting equality until 1928.

POLITICS IN WRITING

I am reminded of four definitions: A Radical is a man with both feet firmly planted – in the air. A Conservative is a man with two perfectly good legs who, however, has never learned to walk forward. A Reactionary is a somnambulist walking backwards. A Liberal is a man who uses his legs and his hands at the behest – at the command – of his head.

Franklin D Roosevelt, US President 1933–1945

QUOTE UNQUOTE

English policy is to float lazily downstream, occasionally putting out a diplomatic boathook to avoid collisions.
Lord Salisbury, Prime Minister 1885–1886, 1886–1892, 1892–1902

POLITICS IN WRITING

I believe that, precisely because of the new fusion between domestic and international politics, intervention in the internal affairs of the state must respond to clearly defined rules and criteria. There needs to be a debate on this point: what are the new rules on the international system of powers? We need to return to a situation in which military action cannot be undertaken by anyone without there being a wide consensus and without it being based on serious justifications. The world cannot function if someone can just say, 'I am strong enough to do what I want, and therefore I will do it.'

Eric Hobsbawm,
The New Century: In conversation with Antonio Polito

ON THE MONEY

One cent (penny)	*Abraham Lincoln (President)*
Five cents (nickel)	*Thomas Jefferson (President)*
Ten cents (dime)	*Franklin Roosevelt (President)*
Twenty-five cents (quarter)	*George Washington (President)*
Fifty cents (half-dollar)	*John F Kennedy (President)*
US \$1 coin (old)	*Susan B Anthony (Campaigner for Reform)*
US \$1 coin (gold)	*Sacagawea (Legendary Native American)*
US \$1 bill	*George Washington (President)*
US \$2 bill	*Thomas Jefferson (President)*
US \$5 bill	*Abraham Lincoln (President)*
US \$10 bill	*Alexander Hamilton (Founding father)*
US \$20 bill	*Andrew Jackson (President)*
US \$50 bill	*Ulysses S Grant (President)*
US \$100 bill	*Benjamin Franklin (Founding father/ Inventor)*
US \$500 bill	*William McKinley (President)*
US \$1000 bill	*Grover Cleveland (President)*
US \$5000 bill	*James Madison (President)*
US \$10,000 bill	*Salmon P Chase (Chief Justice)*
US \$100,000 bill	*Woodrow Wilson (President)*

MAYOR FOR EVER

Frenchman Edmond Mathis was one of the oldest mayors in the world. He died in office at the age of 101 in 1953. He was also the longest-serving mayor – he was elected in 1878 in Ehuns, France, when he was 26. The youngest mayor elected was Shane Mack, who was only 18 years and 169 days old when he was elected at Castlewood, South Dakota in 1988.

94 *Year in the eighteenth century when rebels liberated Haiti from French and British colonialists after a slave revolt three years earlier*

CUPBOARD LOVE

There are various ways and means to get yourself elected as a party or an MP, but surely none better than those adopted by Sir William Paxton, who ran for the seat of Carmarthenshire in the general election of 1802. Recently returned from India and wishing to establish himself in this country, his campaign involved spending £15,690 4s 2d on booze and food for his electorate. Over the 15 days of polling, he apparently paid for:

11,070 breakfasts
36,901 dinners
684 suppers
11,068 bottles of spirits
25,275 gallons of ale
8,879 bottles of porter
460 bottles of sherry
509 bottles of cider
4,521 charges for horse hire

The sting in the tale is that he lost the election by 1,267 votes to 1,222. However, he got in the following year as MP for the borough seat of Carmarthen. Which may have been how long it took the voters to recover from the party.

QUOTE UNQUOTE

I hate liberality – nine times out of ten it is cowardice,
and the tenth time lack of principle.
Henry Addington, Prime Minister 1801–1804

THE RULES OF THE HOUSE

Like Bill Clinton and Fidel Castro after him, Winston Churchill was partial to a cigar. But MPs have been banned from smoking in the Chamber and during any of the House's proceedings, including committees, since 1693. MPs and officers of the House are still provided with snuff from the doorkeeper's box near the entrance to the Chamber. The small wooden box is made from timber that fell from the ceiling when bombs hit the Palace of Westminster during World War Two, and the names of the doorkeepers are engraved on the box's brass plaque. The tradition is believed to be a hangover from around two hundred years ago, when the snuff helped to weaken the smell of the remains of slaughtered sheep and cattle floating in the Thames (Westminster Bridge was used to transport livestock to a nearby market). During the mid-nineties at least one MP, who shall remain nameless, took snuff. The practice is thought to have cost the taxpayer 87p per year.

Margaret Thatcher was a research chemist, Tony Blair a barrister. William Hague worked as a management consultant and Iain Duncan Smith was in the army. There is no one sure way to get into politics and no such thing as a professional politician, although a safe seat helps to secure political longevity. Politicians often don't go straight into politics – Tony Blair was not elected to Parliament until he was 30.

Politics degrees, political activities at school or university and involvement at youth parliaments and with political parties can all help, but even university is not a pre-requisite. John Major didn't go. And would-be Labour MPs from public schools should not despair. Being a former public school boy didn't stop Blair. The Prime Minister went to Fettes, 'the Scottish Eton', a fee-paying school, whereas former Tory leader Hague went to a state comprehensive in West Yorkshire.

There is an almost infinite variety of paths into politics. But some jobs are more obviously political than others, such as a position in the Clerk's Department in the House of Commons or the Parliament Office in the Lords. Clerks draft reports, attend meetings and provide advice. Each House also has its own library department. Graduates without professional library qualifications can become library clerks and train on the job. Librarians respond to requests from individual Members and prepare briefing papers on any topic relevant to parliamentary concern. Then there are Think Tanks. Some are independent, while others, such as the Institute of Public Policy Research, adopt a particular political position (in their case, centre left). The Directory of Think Tank Publications provides a list of internships and gives addresses of the relevant organisations.

Political consultancy is also a good way in. Consultants lobby on behalf of their clients and use their contacts to arrange meetings and presentations. Working for an MP is another well-trodden path. All MPs have an allowance to pay researchers, and because MPs' budgets don't always match their workloads, offers of unpaid assistance can be well received. Would-be politicians can also get involved in pressure groups, trade unions and political parties. Most party political activity in the UK is carried out by volunteers rather than paid staff. There is always extra work to be done come election time.

But then comes the hard part. Becoming an MP involves selection by a political party and then by the electorate. Being a woman is no longer as big an obstacle to election as it once was; 119 women were elected to Parliament in 1997 compared to 23 in 1983. The main thing to remember is that there are only 659 seats in the House of Commons. Only the really committed need apply.

THE OLD SYSTEM

Before the people were given the vote, things were a bit different...

King – owned all the land. Would grant parcels of land in return for the promise of future service.

Lords/overlords – held land given to them by the king, which they leased in return for the pledge of financial aid or the use of their knights.

Vassals – Barons who paid homage to the overlords and leased land to Knights.

Knights – sometimes sub-tenants of vassals, rented land in return for services rendered.

Squires – trainee knights, aged 14 to 21 years old.

Seigneurs – Lords of a manor, a manor being the smallest parcel of land.

Villeins/serfs – tied to their fief or manor, they worked for the lord and paid him rent.

Servants – owned by the nobility and wealthy merchants.

POLITICAL ANAGRAMS

Of which QC is this an anagram
I'M NOT HARSH ON MANDY
Answer on page 153.

FROM SPORT TO POLITICS

Footballers are not usually known for their political ambitions, so it is all the more surprising when one hangs up his boots to pursue a career in politics. Belgian footballer Marc Wilmots swapped the captain's armband for political power when he was elected to the Belgian Senate with 79,437 votes. Wilmots skippered Belgium in the 2002 World Cup in Japan, scoring a disallowed goal against tournament winners Brazil, before being tempted into politics. As a member of the MR, the French-speaking Liberal Party, he was given an informal role as sports ambassador to the people.

Wilmots followed in the hallowed footsteps of Pele, the greatest footballer of them all, who reached high office in Brazil. But success on the pitch doesn't always bring success at the dispatch box. While he may have captained Pakistan to glory in the 1991 cricket World Cup, Imran Khan's Justice Party didn't win a single seat in the 1997 elections. He was elected to the Pakistani parliament in 2002.

REPORTING POLITICS

Chris Moncrieff, lobby journalist, on how to get the scoop

Never argue with MPs when they start spouting their policies. Just nod as if in agreement so that Members of all parties will assume you are one of them. Scour the Order Paper for quirky questions or motions and contact the MP involved. There is often a story to be had. Collect MPs' phone numbers with the avidity that George V collected stamps. Get your face known by going to the Members' Lobby whenever the opportunity occurs and just wait around like a prostitute soliciting for business. Which is what you are doing. You will find that as MPs get to know you and see you there, they will often put you on the trail of a story. You very rarely return from the Lobby empty-handed. And never breach a confidence – the word will soon get round and you will be treated like a pariah. And remember: more stories come out of the Palace of Westminster than any other building in the land.

OLD SCHOOL TIES

Arthur Wellesley, Duke of Wellington, who became Prime Minister in 1828, was the first PM not to have attended either Oxford or Cambridge university (excluding William Cavendish, the Duke of Devonshire, who had a private education, so doesn't count). He was, however, hardly uneducated: he attended Brown's Seminary in Chelsea, Eton and the Brussels and Angers Military Academy.

While the number of PMs with an Oxbridge pedigree are still in the majority, a few Prime Ministers have broken the educational mould. Some more radically than others.

John Russell (PM 1846–1852, 1865–1866) went to Westminster and Edinburgh University

Benjamin Disraeli (PM 1868, 1874–1880) studied at Lincoln's Inn

David Lloyd George (PM 1916–1922) went to Llanystumdwy Church School

Andrew Bonar Law (PM 1922–1923) went to Gilbertfield in Hamilton & Glasgow High School

James Ramsay MacDonald (PM in 1924 and 1929–1935) went to Drainie Parish Board School

Neville Chamberlain (PM 1937–1940) went to Rugby and Mason College (later Birmingham University)

Winston Churchill (PM 1940–1945, 1951–1955) went to Harrow and Sandhurst

James Callaghan (PM 1976–1979) went to state school in Portsmouth

John Major (PM 1990–1997) went to Rutlish Grammar School

Year, in the nineteenth century, when Queen Liliuokalani of Hawaii, was forced to stand down after the island was annexed by the US

WHO'S IN THE HOUSE?

The main UK political parties currently occupying the House of Commons, in order of the number of seats won at the General Election in May 2001...

Labour Party...**413**

Conservative and Unionist Party **166**
Liberal Democrats **52**

Ulster Unionist Party **6**

Scottish National Party..**5**

Democratic Unionist Party **5**

Plaid Cymru **4**

Sinn Fein **4**

SDLP **3**

British National Party..**0**

Green Party **0**

United Kingdom Independence Party.............................**0**

QUOTE UNQUOTE

When I am right, I get angry. Churchill gets angry when he is wrong. We are angry at each other much of the time.
Charles de Gaulle, first President of Fifth French Republic, 1959–1969, on Winston Churchill

---

POLITICS IN WRITING

But now, Oedipus, mightiest in the sight of all, all we suppliants implore you to find some protection for us, whether your knowledge comes from hearing a message from a god or from a man, perhaps; for I see that the setting together of counsels is most effective for those who have experience. Come, best of living men, raise up the city! Come, take care! For now this land calls you its preserver on account of the energy you showed before; and let it not be our memory of your reign that we were stood up straight at first only to fall later; no, raise up the city so that it does not fall! The good fortune you gave us before came with a favourable omen; be the same now! For if you are to continue ruling, as you govern now, better rule a land that has men than one that is empty, since a wall or ship is nothing without men who live inside it.

Sophocles, *Oedipus Tyrannus*

Percentage of Gibraltans who voted not to share British sovereignty with 99 Spain in 2002

The **Anarchist Pogo Party of Germany** took part in the Bundestag elections in 1998, the main thrust of its policy being free beer for voters. Members were encouraged to chant the party slogan of 'work is shit'.

The **Ezenhemmer Plastic Bags and Child Rearing Utensils Party** (or Ezen) is a Swedish party consisting of 72 members formed in reaction to 'the world-wide, dead boring, political seriousness'. Everyone should be more cheerful, according to Ezen, instead of engaging in disputes with opponents. Then everybody would feel a lot better and be in harmony with the rest of the world. Ezen's leader is the mysterious KM. Even within the party his identity is debated – some believe him to be the pet black cat of one of Ezen's founders.

Legalise Cannabis Alliance (LCA): Their goal is to legalise cannabis, to encourage increased utilisation of cannabis and its products 'for the betterment of society and the world', and the release of all prisoners convicted of cannabis offences (only).

The **New Sensual Power Party** – George W Bush may have sent troops to Iraq but one presidential candidate thought the US should have sent hookers instead. Clint Arthur said he had a platform based on the philosophy, 'make love, not war'. Arthur said the US could easily overthrow Saddam Hussein by sending hordes of prostitutes – or 'goddesses' – to the Middle East to teach the locals how to 'physically pleasure each other'. If elected, Arthur's inaugural speech would have explained how to give a woman multiple orgasms – information he believes will revitalize the economy better than any tax plan.

The **Rock 'n' Roll Loony Party** was formed as an off-shoot of The Monster Raving Loony Party after the death of Screaming Lord Sutch. In the Swale Borough Council Elections (2003) one of its candidates won more votes than a member of the Liberal Democrat Party. The leader is called 'Screwy Driver'.

The **Natural Law Party** (UK) is no longer a registered party but still campaigns on the basis that it can provide 'the knowledge through which human life can be raised to the same level of perfection with which Natural Law eternally governs the entire universe'. The establishment of 'a group of 7,000 experts practising Maharishi's Transcendental Meditation and TM-Sidhi programme, including the technique of Yogic Flying' has been identified as a party priority upon election.

INCA EMPERORS 1200 TO 1572

Kingdom of Cuzco

Established around 1200 after Manco Capac led ten Inca clans from Lake Titicaca in northern Peru to conquer the fertile plains in the south. The battle was won and Cuzco was founded.

c.1200–1400 (Specific dates for this period unknown)
Manco Capac (a mythical figure, but central to Inca history)
Sinchi Roca • Lloque Yupanqui
Mayta Capac • Capac Yupanqui
Inca Roca • Yahuar Huacadc • Viracocha Inca

The Empire

A period of rapid expansion for the Inca Empire which at it's height spread from northern Ecuador to central Chile. Rapid 'civilisation' followed which included the development of a system of government and a state religion.

1438–71 Pachacuti • 1471–1493 Topa Inca
1493–1528 Huayna Capac • 1528–1532 Huascar
1532–1533 Atahualpa

Vilcabamba State

Vilcabamba was the Inca's last stronghold against the Spanish conquistadors. An inhospitable region of jungles and mountains, Vilcabamba State was finally taken in 1572.

1533 Topa Hualpa • 1533–1545 Manco Inca
1545–1560 Sayri Tupac • 1560–1571 Titu Cusi Yupanqui
1571–1572 Tupac Amaru

POLITICAL ANAGRAMS

Of which Law Lord is this an anagram?
NO, DON'T HURT BLAIR
Answer on page 153.

IT'S A SCANDAL

In 1892 Edward Samuel Wesley de Cobain, the MP for Belfast East, a nonconformist and stalwart of the Orange Order, was charged with committing an act of gross indecency with another man. De Cobain took refuge in the US and when summoned to attend the Commons, he failed to show and was expelled. He later quietly returned to Belfast, but the police soon found him at his home. On 21 March, 1893, de Cobain was convicted and sentenced to 12 months in jail with hard labour.

Number of up-to-date mobile phones stolen in the House of Commons over four years to 2002 101

*'If you can't float like a butterfly or sting like a bee,
then at least floor him with one of your John Prescott's!'*

QUOTE UNQUOTE

Loyalty is a fine quality, but in excess it fills political graveyards.
Neil Kinnock, Leader of the Labour Party 1983–1992

HATS OFF

When the House rises at the end of a session in the Commons, the policemen on duty shout, 'Who goes home?' This is not the beginning of a party game, nor an invitation to share a cab. It is a tradition stemming from a time when members were urged to leave in groups to cross the dangerous, unlit fields between Westminster and the City. They would also club together to hire boats home on the Thames.

When the Speaker leaves his chair at the end of a session, he says to the Sergeant on duty, 'Usual time tomorrow,' or, if it is after midnight, 'Usual time this day.' As he then processes out and into the central lobby the inspector on duty there shouts, 'Hats off, strangers' – at which point anyone wearing a hat should remove it, including the policemen. The House of Commons is currently trying to ban the term 'strangers'.

PINK PARADE

The largest gay and lesbian rights march in history took place near the Washington Memorial in the US capital on April 25, 1993. Estimates of attendance range from 300,000 to one million. The gathering demanded equal rights for homosexuals. There were calls for anti-discrimination regulations and an end to the ban on homosexuals in the US military.

LICENCE TO KILL

Andrew Jackson became the only President to kill someone in a duel when he shot dead a man named Charles Dickinson in 1806. Jackson took offence when Dickinson insulted his wife – Jackson's wife, that is. Dickinson was one of the best shots in Tennessee and had choice of weapons. He chose pistols and got his shot away first, hitting the rib cage of the future president. Jackson held steady, however, despite having two broken ribs and Dickinson had to stand at the mark and await his fate. Jackson hit his adversary full in the stomach. Although duelling was judged acceptable at the time, many considered the killing to have been in cold blood.

WHY YOU SHOULD STAY OUT OF POLITICS

Leading criminal and public inquiries barrister, Michael Mansfield QC, on why he didn't go into politics...

'Power tends to corrupt and absolute power corrupts absolutely.' I have always regarded this as axiomatic with respect to political life and the performance of the two main parties in Westminster over the last three decades bears clear witness to it.

The Parliamentary path is littered with broken promises and the tarnished spangles of real politik or the Third Way. Even Billy Elliot couldn't match the number of volte face and pirouettes. Anyone daring to don the mantle of principle is promptly shunted into the wings and branded, at best naive, at worst deluded.

For me, change is forged by the force of ordinary people joining together over issues about which they feel strongly. If this is done with commitment, perseverance and determination, it creates both a threat and a risk to the retention of power by those who temporarily hold the reins. Fine recent examples of this are provided by Doreen and Neville Lawrence; and the many families involved in the Marchioness disaster, the various Rail Inquiries, Bloody Sunday amd Omagh.

For the House of Lords, the annual Queen's Speech is a chance to lord it over the Commons. While they sit comfortably, the Commons are required to stand at the Bar of the House of Lords – traditionally the senior chamber.

Otherwise known as the Royal Address, the speech can be traced back to 1536. Its modern form dates from the opening of the present Palace of Westminster in 1852.

In anticipation of the royal procession, the Imperial State Crown, the Sword of State and the Cap of Maintenance are taken to Westminster by coach. The Household Cavalry escort the monarch from Buckingham Palace, down The Mall and along Whitehall to the Lords. The procession ends as it passes through the Royal Arch of the Victoria Tower. Before she enters the chamber, the Queen dons her royal robes in the robing room.

Meanwhile an unfortunate government whip is, according to custom, held 'hostage' back at Buckingham Palace to guarantee the safe return of the monarch. The tradition is a throwback to a time when relations between Parliament and the monarchy could be strained.

The size of the Queen's procession was trimmed in 1998, but officers of state, including the Lord Great Chamberlain, still lead the column and face the monarch by walking backwards. This ensures that no disrespect is shown. In a magnanimous gesture, the palace recently offered the leaders the choice of walking forwards, but they declined.

The chamber rises as the Queen enters and the lighting is turned up to embellish the spectacle. The Gentleman Usher of the Black Rod, an official of the Royal Household, meanwhile knocks on the door of the Commons three times with his ebony stick to summon MPs to the Lords. The door is at first slammed in his face, which emphasises the Commons' independence from the monarchy.

However, they then open up, hear his summons, and shuffle reluctantly to the Upper House. After the Lord Chancellor has handed the Queen her speech, she delivers it from the throne in the Lords. The Royal Address is in fact not the Queen's work at all. It is written by the government to announce their legislative plans for the next parliament.

Later in the day the Commons and Lords move a Loyal Address in answer to the Speech. A debate follows and then the politicians are allowed to get on with their work.

About ten days ago, I retired very late. I had been up waiting for important dispatches from the front. I could not have been long in bed when I fell into a slumber, for I was weary. I soon began to dream. There seemed to be a death-like stillness about me. Then I heard subdued sobs, as if a number of people were weeping. I thought I left my bed and wandered downstairs. There the silence was broken by the same pitiful sobbing, but the mourners were invisible. I went from room to room; no living person was in sight, but the same mournful sounds of distress met me as I passed along. I saw light in all the rooms; every object was familiar to me; but where were all the people who were grieving as if their hearts would break? I was puzzled and alarmed. What could be the meaning of all this? Determined to find the cause of a state of things so mysterious and so shocking, I kept on until I arrived at the East Room, which I entered. There I met with a sickening surprise. Before me was a catafalque, on which rested a corpse wrapped in funeral vestments. Around it were stationed soldiers who were acting as guards; and there was a throng of people, gazing mournfully upon the corpse, whose face was covered, others weeping pitifully. 'Who is dead in the White House?' I demanded of one of the soldiers, 'The President,' was his answer; 'he was killed by an assassin.' Then came a loud burst of grief from the crowd, which woke me from my dream. I slept no more that night; and although it was only a dream, I have been strangely annoyed by it ever since.'

Abraham Lincoln's dream three days before he was assassinated on 14 April 1865

Ward Hill Lamon, *Recollections of Abraham Lincoln 1847–1865*

PRESIDENTIAL SCANDALS

Franklin Roosevelt's wife Eleanor discovered her husband's affair with Lucy Mercer in 1918 when she found some love letters from Lucy to her husband while emptying his suitcase after a European trip. Lucy was Eleanor's social secretary at the time when Roosevelt served as Assistant Secretary to the Navy. Roosevelt turned down his wife's offer of a divorce. Although he agreed to end the romance, it began again and continued while he was President. Lucy would visit the White House when Eleanor was away and Roosevelt dispatched a private car for his mistress and organised for her to have a front row seat at his inauguration. Lucy was with Roosevelt when he died of a cerebral haemorrhage in Warm Springs, Georgia in 1945. Like the affair itself, this was not made public until much later. Eleanor arrived later and discovered that Lucy had taken her place at her husband's side.

A mass political boycott of the 1980 Moscow Olympics plunged the games into a Cold War crisis. In 1979 the Soviet Union had invaded Afghanistan and the Olympics became the international focus of the conflict. President Jimmy Carter called for the US team to boycott the games after the International Olympic Committee refused to relocate them.

Carter later said: 'It should be remembered that in the United States and other free countries, the national Olympic committees were independent of government control'. But Carter had promised to revoke the passports of any US athletes who chose to compete.

The British Olympic Association voted against the government and decided to send athletes to the Games. The BOA Chairman Sir Dennis Follows said, 'We believe sport should be a bridge, and not a destroyer.' US allies France, Italy and Sweden also took part. But around 60 countries boycotted the games and the athletes of only 81 countries ran, jumped or swam for the record books.

In a severely reduced field, the USSR won 197 medals, 80 of them gold.

The USSR tried to get its own back in 1984 by boycotting the Los Angeles games. The official line was that it feared for its athletes' safety in what was referred to as an anti-Communist environment. But the move was widely seen as an act of revenge for the 1980 games.

This time 140 countries took part – a record attendance for an Olympics – and the games were the first since 1932 to record a profit. Even Communist China returned to the Olympic fold in Los Angeles after a 32-year absence.

IT'S A SCANDAL

In January 1721, John Aislabie, MP for Ripon, resigned as Chancellor of the Exchequer after the bursting of the South Sea Bubble. He had overseen an agreement whereby the South Sea Company took over the national debt. A parliamentary investigation had found that he had accepted a large amount of stock as payment for recommending the scheme to the House. The Commons found him guilty of 'the most notorious, dangerous and infamous corruption'. He was expelled from the House and sent to prison, serving his term in the Tower of London. After his release, Aislabie, who had inherited the Studley estate in 1693, took to tending his gardens again. He created the water garden at Studley Royal and was the first English natural landscape gardener.

The Government's draconian pocket-money tax forced some children to take the law into their own hands.

HOW DID THEY VOTE?

In a series of referendums in 2003, nine European countries voted on whether or not to join the EU on 1 May 2004. But how keen were they?

Country	Voted to join	Turnout	Population
Slovakia	92.46%	52.15%	5.4 million
Lithuania	91.04%	63,3%	3.4 million
Slovenia	89.61%	60.29%	2 million
Hungary	83.76%	45.62%f	9.9 million
Poland	77.45%	58.85%	38.6 million
Czech Rep	77.33%	55.21%	10.2 million
Latvia	67%	72.53%	2.3 million
Estonia	66.92%	64%	1.3 million
Malta	53.65%	91%	394,000

The 10th new member, Cyprus, held a different referendum, which was to decide whether or not it could reunify its Turkish and Greek halves before joining the EU. In April 2004, the Turkish Cypriots voted yes, but the Greek Cypriots voted to remain divided, as they disagreed with the UN reunification plan. Cyprus duly joined the EU in 2004, but the EU laws and benefits apply only to the Greek half of Cyprus.

The number of seats in the Reichstag won by the Nazi Party in 1930

Political leaders assassinated or executed

Park Chung Hee
President of South Korea
26 October 1979
– 'accidentally' shot by his chief of intelligence service Kim Jea Kyu.

Zulfikar Ali Bhutto
Pakistan Prime Minister
4 April 1979
– executed (hanged).

Anwar Sadat
President of Egypt
6 October 1981
– two grenades went off, following which gunmen opened fire with machine guns while the President was watching an aerial display at a military parade. A number of others were killed.

Benigno Aquino
Philippines opposition leader
21 August 1983
– shot on his return from exile. He told reporters: 'My feeling is we all have to die sometime and if it's my fate to die by an assassin's bullet, so be it.'

Nicolae Ceausescu
Romanian President
25 December 1989
– executed (he and his wife Elena were shot by firing squad).

Rajiv Gandhi
former Indian Prime Minister
21 May 1991
– killed while campaigning in the world's largest democratic election when a bomb hidden in a basket of flowers exploded.

SLAVE LABOUR

At the time of Augustus, it is thought that out of a population of around 900,000, 300,000-350,000 were slaves. Roman society relied heavily on slavery. Without it, empire would have been implausible, the economy unsustainable. But the huge slave population had to be carefully managed. The lure of freedom was a powerful instrument of political control.

Slaves could be liberated through 'manumission vindicta' (where a magistrate touched the manumitted, or freed, slave with a rod – vindicta) or 'testamento' (by will). If the manumittor was a Roman citizen, the 'freedman' would become a Roman citizen too – but with only limited rights. Many 'freedmen' didn't have citizens' rights at all.

A consensual process involving master and state was needed for the slaves to be freed and Imperial Rome was careful to monitor the integration of ex-slaves into its citizen body to avoid any kind of civil unrest. Only when there was a population crisis were the rules relaxed. Emperor Caracalla liberally extended the citizenship to all free-born early in 212 AD.

POLITICS IN POETRY

Fie politics, go wear a whiter shroud!
Your clothes are stained by blood of many men;
No nation seems to be of you quite proud;
Your tongue has lied and falsely signed your pen.
Your hands have been receiving bribes for long;
There is not much reprieve for common man;
All empty promises have been your song;
When will your services become yeoman?
O politics! Refurbish your makeup!
Be transparent, honest and just in life;
With friend corruption, always you go sup;
Money when earned by fraudulence brings strife.
Fie politics! Recount your past blunders;
Before the wrath of God on you thunders.

Dr John Celes, Sonnet: 'Politics Personified'

POLITICAL ANAGRAMS

Of what US policy is this an anagram?
REQUIRING CONTRACTS
Answer on page 153.

QUOTE UNQUOTE

*It is a pity, as my husband says, that more politicians are not
bastards by birth instead of vocation.*
Katherine Whitehorn, journalist

ASSASSINATION ATTEMPTS

On 30 March 1981, President Ronald Reagan, who hadn't been in office for long, must have wished he had stuck to the movies. When Reagan left the Washington Hilton Hotel, about a mile from the White House, after addressing a union convention on the 69th day of his presidency, a 26-year-old bystander called John Hinckley Jr discharged his .22 pistol from close range. He hit the President in the chest. Reagan underwent emergency surgery at the George Washington University Hospital and almost died, but instead survived and went on to serve two terms. Three other men were wounded in the attack. The White House Press Secretary James Brady was hit in the head and a Secret Service official and a Washington policeman were also injured before police forced Hinckley to the ground. Hinckley claimed he had staged the attack to impress film star Jodie Foster, with whom he was obsessed. He was later declared insane and sent to a high-security mental hospital.

In the winter of 1964, Nelson Rolihlahla Mandela stepped on to Robben Island, South Africa's notorious prison, to begin his sentence. He was to spend 26 years in prison, most of them on an outcrop off the coast of the Western Cape. He was allowed just one visitor every six months for 30 minutes and could send and receive a letter only every six months. The floor was his bed, he had a bucket for a toilet, and from these humble surroundings he led the symbolic fight against segregation.

Apartheid laws enacted in 1948 institutionalised racial discrimination in South Africa. Race laws prohibited marriage between non-whites and whites, and sanctioned 'white-only' jobs. The Population Registration Act of 1950 required all South Africans to be classified as white, black (African), or coloured (of mixed descent).

Born in the village of Qunu in the Transkei on 18 July 1918, Mandela joined the African National Congress in 1942 while studying to become a lawyer. He was elected National Volunteer-in-Chief of the ANC when it launched the Campaign for the Defiance of Unjust Laws in 1952. During the 1950s, Mandela was banned, arrested and imprisoned. He was one of the accused in the Treason Trial that eventually collapsed in 1961. After the Sharpeville Massacre in 1960 when 69 blacks were killed after a civil rights protest, the ANC was outlawed. When the government ignored his calls for a democratic constitution, Mandela went into hiding. Disguised sometimes as a chauffeur, sometimes as a labourer, he helped form the Umkhonto we Sizwe in 1961. The armed wing of the ANC marked a new, non-peaceful stage of resistance. Mandela later explained that he had turned to violent means 'only when all else had failed'.

At the Rivonia Trial (1963–1964), Mandela stood accused of sabotage designed to 'ferment violent revolution'. He conducted his own defence. He claimed he had no duty to obey the laws of a white parliament in which he was not represented. His statement from the dock ended: 'I have cherished the ideal of a democratic and free society in which all persons live together in harmony and with equal opportunities. It is an ideal which I hope to live for and to achieve. But if needs be, it is an ideal for which I am prepared to die.' He was sentenced to life imprisonment.

During Mandela's years behind bars there was an international campaign for his release. On 11 February 1990, he walked free and greeted the waiting crowd. On 10 May 1994 he was inaugurated as the first democratically elected State President of South Africa. Apartheid had finally bent to the force of his will.

The men who helped to cast off the imperial shackles from the Latin American states...

José Gervasio Artigas
1764–1850 Uruguay

Simón Bolívar *1783–1830*
Venezuela, Colombia, Bolivia, Ecuador, Peru, Panama

Jean-Pierre Boyer *1776–1850*
Haiti

Henry Christophe *1767–1820*
Haiti

Jean-Jacques Dessalines
1758–1806 Haiti

Juan José Flores *1800–1864*
Ecuador

Juan Antonio Lavalleja
1784-1853 Uruguay

Francisca de Miranda
1750–1816 Venezuela

Bernardo O'Higgins *1778-1842*
Chile

José Antonio Páez *1790–1873*
Venezuela

Pedro I *1826–1831*
Brazil

José Fructuoso Rivera
1784–1854 Uruguay

General José de San Martín
1778–1850 Chile, Peru

Franciso de Paula Santander
1792–1840
Colombia (New Granada)

General Antonio José de Sucre
1795–1830 Ecuador, Bolivia

Dominique Toussaint
L'Ouverture *1743–1803* Haiti

CROSSING THE FLOOR

In 1995 Alan Howarth became the first Tory MP to 'cross the floor' of the House in order to join the Labour Party. Howarth had been the Conservative MP for Stratford-on-Avon since 1983 and had held various ministerial positions. He was not a member of government at the time of the switch, but his defection was seen as a blow to John Major's administration. His constituents then found themselves in the unusual position of being represented by a party for which they had not voted. Howarth won the Welsh seat of Newport East in 1997 as New Labour swept to power. Tony Blair appointed him as Employment Minister and in 1998 Howarth became Minister for the Arts.

Back in 1904, Winston Churchill crossed the floor to leave the Conservatives and join the Liberal Party. He returned to the Conservatives in the 1920s.

Time in years between the Labour Party first pledging its support for home rule 111
in Scotland (1888) and Labour establishing the Scottish parliament (1999)

THE WIG'S THE THING

Tradition used to demand that the Lord Chancellor go about his daily chores in the House of Lords in a full-bottomed wig, tights, breeches and buckled shoes. But in 1998, the then Lord Chancellor, Lord Irvine, complained to the Procedure Committee about the tradition, which dated back to the seventeenth century. Of his post-Reformation attire, he moaned, 'The wig weighs an absolute ton. It is very uncomfortable.'

Lord Irvine is clearly not of the same disposition as Sir Chistopher Hatton, the first Chancellor dressed in such robes in a portrait and a man famed for 'his taste in dress and skill in dancing'. Many peers voted against the idea of change. Tory Peer Earl Ferrers said the Lord Chancellor 'should not dispose of his breeches, buttons and tights.' (The remark paints an alarming picture of a naked Chancellor.) But Lord Irvine's proposals that he wear the Lord Chancellor's gown, coat jacket, and ruffled collar, with ordinary black shoes and trousers were accepted by 145 votes to 115.

INSIDE CENTRAL GOVERNMENT

George I was German and couldn't speak much English and by all accounts he wasn't much interested in politics, either. In those circumstances, chairing the Cabinet as Sovereign would have been tricky, so he handed the responsibility over to the First Lord of the Treasury, Sir Robert Walpole. As the most important minister during the 1721–1724 government, Walpole became known as the first Prime Minister. Today, the Queen appoints as Prime Minister the leader of the party that has a majority in the House of Commons. The formal office of the Prime Minister is unpaid, but the offices of First Lord of the Treasury and Minister for the Civil Service, which the Prime Minister also undertakes, are rather well paid.

Among many other functions, the Prime Minister has to chair Cabinet meetings, appoint and allocate roles to Ministers and appoint the archbishop of the Church of England, as well as senior judges and even the Poet Laureate. The Prime Minister is often referred to as 'primus inter pares' – first among equals – although how equal the Prime Minister feels to the Cabinet depends on his or her relationship with them, which can vary from close to indifferent. Nevertheless, the power of a Prime Minister is kept in check by the PM's need to maintain support among ministers and backbenchers. The weaker the Parliamentary majority of a government, the more attention a Prime Minister must pay to the views of backbenchers.

---

112 *The number of seats in Ukraine's 450 seat Parliament won by pro-Western reform party Our Ukraine in 2002*

*I remain just one thing, and one thing only – and that is a clown.
It places me on a far higher plane than any politician.*
Charlie Chaplin, actor and director

ASSASSINATION ATTEMPTS

Adolf Hitler escaped with an injured arm after an assassination attempt by Colonel Claus von Stauffenberg on 20 July, 1944. The colonel had become disillusioned with the Nazi regime and concealed a bomb in a briefcase. The Nazi leader was holding a meeting with staff in 'the Wolf's Lair', his headquarters near Rastenburg, when the bomb exploded. Four men were killed but the heavy oak conference table protected the Führer. The plan had been for various military figures including Friedrich Fromm, the chief of armaments, to assume control of the German Army. Fromm had not opposed the plot but in an attempt to save himself, he organised the executions of Claus von Stauffenberg and two other conspirators, Friedrich Olbricht and Werner von Haeften. Stauffenberg reportedly died shouting 'Long live free Germany'. They were not the only ones to die – 5,000 Germans were executed after the assassination attempt. Hitler arranged for the leaders to suffer a slow death. They were hung from meat-hooks with piano wire. Film footage of the executions was presented to senior members of the Nazi Party and the armed forces.

POLITICS IN WRITING

We have learned that we cannot live alone, at peace; that our own well-being is dependent on the well-being of other nations, far away. We have learned that we must live as men, and not as ostriches, not as dogs in the manger. We have learned to be citizens of the world, members of the human community.

Franklin D Roosevelt, US President 1933–1945,
fourth inaugural address

HAVE CAMEL, WILL VOTE

Staging elections in a country the size of India poses major logistical problems. In the 2004 election, voting had to be completed in phases to allow the officials and security workers to move from area to area. Helicopters, camels, elephants and yaks were pressed into service to help the officials complete their enormous task. In one constituency, a landslide interrupted polling. The election lasted three weeks.

THE EVITA LEGACY

During the 2001 economic crash in Argentina, provincial governments ran out of pesos with which to pay their workers. Instead of cash, employees were given bonds that depicted the Argentine heroine Eva Perón. Born Maria Eva Duarte, Eva married Colonel Juan Domingo Perón in 1945. After her husband was elected President in June 1946 she became a champion of the working classes. Known affectionately as Evita, she helped gain women the vote for the first time and won equal rights for illegitimate children. She was adored by millions, but hated by the anti-Peronist middle classes who saw her as a populist.

Evita died of cancer on 26 July 1952. The official statement from the Subsecretariat of Information read: 'It is our sad duty to inform the people of the Republic that Eva Perón, the Spiritual Leader of the Nation, died at 8.25pm.' Millions of Argentines lined the streets at her funeral. Her body was embalmed, before being taken on a tour of European countries. She now rests in La Recoleta, a cemetery in Buenos Aires. The words 'Don't cry for me, Argentina, I remain very near you' are inscribed on her tomb. Evita's influence lives on and the government bonds printed in 2001 were popularly known as 'Evitas'.

IT'S A SCANDAL

In 1967, Tory peer and novelist Lord Archer won damages of £500,000 against the *Daily Star* after the paper accused him of sleeping with a prostitute. But his case had relied on faked diary entries and the false alibi of Ted Francis, his friend at the time. In November 1999 Francis came clean about his account of a night in 1986 in the *News of the World*, and the millionaire author found himself standing trial for perjury and perverting the course of justice.

Archer was found guilty and sentenced to four years in prison. The judge, Mr Justice Potts, told Archer: 'These charges represent as serious an offence of perjury as I have had experience of and have been able to find in the books... It has been an extremely distasteful case.' Newspapers were delighted – none more so than the *Daily Star*. The tabloid led with the headline 'Pay us £2.2 million'. It quoted the title of one of Archer's novels, announcing it wanted 'not a penny more not a penny less'.

However, despite his disgrace, Archer retained his peerage. A House of Lords spokesman explained: 'There is no precedent for a life peerage being removed. I think treason would be the only exception.' Archer was, though, stripped of the Tory whip in the House, and William Hague announced, 'This is the end of politics for Jeffrey Archer. I will not tolerate behaviour like this in my party.'

POLITICS IN WRITING

So the son of Peleus spoke, and he threw the staff to the ground, studded with its golden nails, and sat down himself. And the son of Atreus kept up his fury on the other side. Then there rose among them Nestor the sweet-spoken, the clear-voiced speaker of Pylos: from his tongue the words flowed sweeter than honey. He had already seen the passing of two generations of humankind, the men who in earlier days had been born and reared with him in Holy Pylos, and now he was ruling over the third. In all good will he spoke and addressed the assembly: 'Oh, shame! Great sorrow is coming on the land of Achaia. There would surely be joy for Priam and his children, and all other Trojans would feel great gladness at heart, if they learnt of all this quarrelling between you two, who are the best of the Danaans in counsel and the best in fighting. No. you must listen to me, since both of you are younger men than I.'

Homer, *Iliad*

QUOTE UNQUOTE

Never believe anything in politics until it has been officially denied.
Otto von Bismarck, German Chancellor 1862–1890

POLITICAL ANAGRAMS

Of what elusive items is this an anagram?
US OWNS MOST... AND ITS FOR PEACE?
Answer on page 153.

RULES OF THE HOUSE

Members are forbidden to die in the House of Commons. Westminster is a Royal Palace, which means that only members of the royal family may breathe their last there. If an MP (or any member of the public) does collapse in the Commons, they are rushed to the nearest hospital, which is St Thomas's, a short walk to the rear of the building. If they die before they leave the Chamber, they are registered as having passed away on the hospital grounds or en route.

EQUAL OPPORTUNITIES

Following the Swedish general election of March 1996, 11 women joined a cabinet of 22 ministers. No other cabinet in the world could match the Social Democratic Party's 50–50 cabinet gender ratio.

There can surely be no other career both so flattering and so frustrating as that of a Member of Parliament. I left my constituency after my election with the feeling that I was nearly as important as people there believed me to be. My maiden speech received a whole column in *The Times* and, as far as I remember some mention in its leader column. Mr. Churchill was one of those who went out of his way to congratulate me. I had been less nervous than I had expected. I seemed to have my foot on the marble staircase that leads up to the Secretary of State's room on the first floor of the Foreign Office.

But a maiden speech is relatively easy, for the Speaker lets you know when he will call you, the tradition of the House is against any interruption, and the following two members are expected – though politically they may hate your guts – to say nice things about your effort. I should have enjoyed the House of Commons more if I had never made a second speech. For, during the second and subsequent speeches there is always the probability that some opponent will leap to his feet with an interruption. You are not compelled to give way, but it is unwise not to do so. His interruption may be irrelevant an idiotic, but it probably succeeds in breaking the thread of you thoughts. If it becomes obvious that it has done so, you may anticipate a whole series of interruptions the next time you catch the Speaker's eye. Even if they are not made, the anticipation of them reduces the confidence with which you face the most difficult audience in the world.

Vernon Bartlett,
And Now, Tomorrow

QUOTE UNQUOTE

*An extraordinary affair. I gave them their orders and
they wanted to stay and discuss them.*
Arthur Wellesley, Duke of Wellington, Prime Minister 1828–1830

REMEMBER ME WHEN I AM GONE, TEDDY

Some leaders are remembered with statues, or have buildings named after them, or streets. President Theodore Roosevelt gave his nickname 'Teddy' to a bear. When he refused to shoot a bear cub while on a hunting trip in Mississippi in 1902, a cartoonist working for the *Washington Post* heard about it and turned the scene into a cartoon for the paper. Boston shopkeeper Morris Michtom then started producing 'Teddy's bears'. Instead of being killed, the original cub went on to be a favourite toy of children around the globe.

A state by state guide to the fall of Communism in Europe

Germany
- *9 November* Berlin Wall breached; formally opened December-January 1990
- *18 March 1990* Free elections in GDR
- *3 October 1990* Reunification of Germany

Czechoslovakia
- *November 1989* Mass demonstrations spread from Prague leading to collapse of Communist rule
- *June 1992* Slovak nationalists win elections in Slovakia
- *1 January 1993* Slovak independence

Poland
- *September 1989* Solidarity-led government takes office
- *January 1990* Communist party dissolves itself
- *October 1991* Free elections under new constitution

Hungary
- *October 1989* Communist rule ends peacefully
- *April/May 1990* Free elections held

Estonia
- *March 1990* Congress of Estonia formed and independence declared
- *September 1991* Independence recognised by USSR

Latvia
- *January 1990* Free elections

- *September 1991* Independence recognised by USSR

Lithuania:
- *March 1990* Declares independence
- *September 1991* Recognised by USSR

Russian Federation
- *June 1991* Boris Yeltsin directly elected president of Russian Federation
- *14 December 1991* Leaders of 10 Union Republics (elected 1990) establish Commonwealth of Independent States (CIS)
- *25 December 1991* USSR ends, Russian Federation its legal successor

Belarus
- *August 1991* Declares independence
- *December 1991* Joins CIS

Ukraine
- *1 December 1991* Referendum vote for independence
- *December 1991* Joins CIS

Romania
- *May 1990* Free elections
- *November 1991* New constitution approved

Bulgaria
- *November 1989* Dictator Zhivkov removed from office
- *June 1990* Free elections

*'And then the prime minister had the audacity to suggest that
the Russians are training dogs as spies...'*

TO COIN A PHRASE

The Iron Curtain divided Europe for almost half a century. According
to the World War Two Field Marshal, Montgomery, in his *History of
Warfare*, it was Winston Churchill who made the term famous.
Churchill sent a telegram on 12 May 1945 to President Truman. In it,
he expressed concern about the future of Europe after the final
surrender by Germany on 7 May 1945 had brought to an end World
War Two. 'I am profoundly concerned about the European situation,'
wrote Churchill, adding, 'An iron curtain is drawn down upon their
front. We do not know what is going on behind.' The significance of
the observation was not lost on Churchill. He later wrote: 'Of all the
public documents I have written on this issue, I would rather be judged
by this.'

When the Iron Curtain came down in 1989–90, the borders between
the two halves of Europe were at last reopened. In 2004, eight former
Soviet states (Poland, Hungary, Czech Republic, Slovakia, Latvia,
Lithuania, Estonia and Slovenia) acceded to the European Union.

While many argue that sport and politics should never mix, South Africa's apartheid regime made it impossible to keep them separate. Under the regime, non-white cricketers were not allowed to play for the national team. The talented batsman Basil D'Oliveira was classified as coloured, so he was compelled to seek international competition elsewhere, and England accepted him. But after hitting a century against Australia in an Ashes Test, he was initially left out of the England team to tour South Africa in 1968. When he was reinstated, the South African Prime Minister, John Vorster, refused to accept what he called a 'political' team, and South Africa was banned from world cricket.

In 1982, Graham Gooch led a rebel cricket tour to South Africa, with a team that included two of D'Oliveira's England team-mates from the 1970s, Geoff Boycott and Alan Knott. The tours were seen to endorse the regime while South Africa was banned from international competition, and were heavily criticised. At the time, the all-white National Party government's Department of Sport spent R3.6 million on white sport, while the Department of Community Development spent a total of R179,000 on black sport. The education budget allocated R913 per white child and R139 per black child.

In 1990, Mike Gatting also led a rebel cricket tour to South Africa, but was forced to return home early after the South African Cricket Union announced that it was to abandon the tour in the name of compromise and conciliation. The pressure from local protests had been immense. Back in England, the anti-apartheid campaigner Peter Hain said: 'Gatting went for the money and his gang is coming back humiliated.'

Politics again intervened in English cricket during the 2003 World Cup. England was due to play a group game against Zimbabwe in Harare. There were calls for the match to be boycotted in protest at the regime of Robert Mugabe. But the government refused to demand England's withdrawal.

Many felt that the cricketers had been abandoned to their consciences. After protracted and emotional talks with the England team, captained by Nasser Hussein, the England and Wales Cricket Board decided not to fulfil their commitment to play the fixture. The decision was made for security and not political reasons, as the team had received a letter containing a death threat from an organisation called the Sons and Daughters of Zimbabwe.

The World Cup technical committee showed the England team little sympathy. It refused to relocate the match to South Africa and England was forced to forfeit all four points. After losing a thrilling encounter to Australia, England was knocked out of the competition.

PRESSURE GROUPS ONLINE

Action on Smoking and Health **www.ash.org**
Amnesty International **www.amnesty.org**
Campaign for Nuclear Disarmament **www.cnduk.org/index.html**
Child Poverty Action Group **www.cpag.org.uk**
Countryside Alliance **www.countryside-alliance.org**
Electoral Reform Society **www.electoral-reform.org.uk**
Fabian Society **www.fabian-society.org.uk**
Free Tibet **www.freetibet.org**
Friends of the Earth **www.foe.co.uk**
Greenpeace **www.greenpeace.org.uk**
Howard League for Penal Reform
www.howardleague.org/index.htm
League Against Cruel Sports **www.league.uk.com**
Shelter **www.shelter.org.uk**
Legalise Cannabis Alliance **www.lca-uk.org**
Liberty **www.liberty-human-rights.org**

QUOTE UNQUOTE

*If you're in politics and you can't tell when you walk into a
room who's for you and who's against you, then you're in
the wrong line of work.*
Lyndon B Johnson, US President 1963–1969

PRESIDENT FOR EVER

Togo is a country of many climates, but few presidents. General
Gnassingbe Eyadema ousted President Nicolas Grunitzky on 14 April
1967 and has been in power ever since. No other President today has
held on to power for so long. Africa's second longest-serving ruler is
Omar Bongo, the president of Gabon. Like Eyadema, Bongo came to
power in 1967. He declared Gabon a one-party state in 1968 (a status
that endured until 1993) and adopted the name of Omar after
converting to Islam in 1973. In early 2004 Bongo was at the centre of
a diplomatic storm between Gabon and Peru when Miss Peru, Ivette
Santa Maria, complained that after her arrival in Gabon to host a
beauty contest she was shown to a room in the presidential palace.
Once inside, the president reportedly pressed a button, doors slid
away and a large bed moved suggestively into view. The Peruvian
ambassador to the United Nations got in touch with his Gabonese
counterpart to articulate his serious concern over the alleged incident.
The claims were subsequently denied by the Gabonese. Santa Maria's
boyfriend was rather confusingly also called Omar.

The libel case that former MP Neil Hamilton brought against businessman Mohammed al-Fayed turned into an unexpectedly bitter struggle, and a huge mistake for Hamilton. A High Court jury unanimously dismissed the former Tory minister's claim that the Egyptian-born Harrods owner had libelled him on the Channel 4 programme 'Dispatches', shown in January 1997. In response, Al-Fayed quipped, 'I was called a Jekyll and Hyde character. There was only one Mr Hyde who tried to hide everything and the jury saw through him.'

In the documentary al-Fayed accused Hamilton of receiving thousands of pounds in cash and other gifts from him in the mid-1980s in return for asking questions in the House of Commons. Hamilton had been the MP for Tatton in Cheshire at the time.

The allegations followed claims made in the *Guardian* in 1994 that Hamilton and another Tory MP, Tim Smith had taken cash for questions. It was revealed that Smith had taken cash from al Fayed and he resigned as a junior Northern Ireland minister.

The jury accepted that al-Fayed had established that Hamilton was corrupt in his capacity as a Member of Parliament. But the Hamiltons remained defiant. Neil denied acting corruptly and said he did not regret taking the action: 'I couldn't have gone through life without straining every sinew within me to bring out the truth.' His ever-loyal wife, Christine, said: 'The jury are wrong is all I want to say – we are not corrupt.' A triumphant al-Fayed was delighted: 'Christmas has come early. This is total vindication.'

YOUNGEST ELECTED US PRESIDENT

Theodore Roosevelt may have been the youngest ever President of the United States, but John Fitzgerald Kennedy was the youngest elected President and the youngest to die in office. Kennedy was elected at the age of 43 in 1960 and was shot dead in Dallas in November 1963. Roosevelt was 42 when he took up residence at the White House following William McKinley's assassination.

POLITICS IN WRITING

Is there any place that is free from evil? It is too simple to say that only the Nazis wanted war...Even good men thought that their private honour would be satisfied by war. They could assert their manhood by killing and being killed. They would accept hardship in recompense for having been selfish and lazy. Danger justified privilege.

Evelyn Waugh, *Unconditional Surrender*

Number of women in the House of Commons by 1998. 71 were newly 121
appointed

Thomas Woodrow Wilson, Theodore Roosevelt and Jimmy Carter are the only US Presidents to have been awarded the Nobel Peace Prize. Woodrow Wilson was rewarded in 1919 for his work as founder of the League of Nations. Carter won the prize in 2002 for his decades of effort to find peaceful solutions to international conflicts, advance democracy and human rights and promote economic and social development. Roosevelt won his for drawing up the 1905 peace treaty between Russia and Japan.

Another American politician to win the prize was Secretary of State Dr Henry Kissinger. He was chosen in 1973 for jointly negotiating the Vietnamese peace accord with Le Duc Tho who declined the prize. Kissinger walked out of a radio interview with Jeremy Paxman during which the interviewer had asked him, 'Did you feel a fraud accepting the Nobel Prize?' Kissinger is thought to have only reluctantly agreed to the interview at all. He accused Paxman of inaccuracy in his questions three times and suggested he had been promised an easy ride. He asked: 'I wonder what you do when you do a hostile interview?'

Sir Austen Chamberlain won the prize as Foreign Minister in 1925 for his role as negotiator of the Locarno Treaty. No British Prime Minister has ever been recognised for their contributions to peace.

The prize was shared in 1994 by the Israeli Prime Minister Yitzhak Rabin, Foreign Minister Shimon Peres and the Chairman of the Executive Committee of the PLO and President of the Palestinian National Authority Yasser Arafat for their efforts to create peace in the Middle East. In 1998, John Hume and David Trimble became Nobel Laureates in recognition of their work for peace in the Northern Ireland.

The Nobel Peace Prize was first awarded in 1901. It is named after Alfred Nobel, a Swedish engineer who invented dynamite. Nobel died on 10 December 1896, but not before he had dedicated part of his fortune to the promotion of peace. In his will, Nobel stated that prizes should be given to those who, during the preceding year 'shall have conferred the greatest benefit on mankind' and that one part be given to the person who 'shall have done the most or the best work for fraternity between nations, for the abolition or reduction of standing armies and for the holding and promotion of peace congresses.'

QUOTE UNQUOTE

My idea of an agreeable person is a person who agrees with me.
Benjamin Disraeli, Prime Minister 1874–1880

The number of rebel Labour MPs who voted against the government in February 2003 over going to war with Iraq

LONGEST SERVING SENATORS

The top 10 longest-serving US senators

Strom Thurmond (Republican-South Carolina), 47 years, five months (retired two weeks before his 100th birthday)

Robert C. Byrd (Democrat-West Virginia), 45 years, three months*

Carl T. Hayden (Democrat-Arizona), 41 years, nine months

Edward M. Kennedy (Democrat-Massachusetts), 41 years, three months*

Daniel K. Inouye (Democrat-Hawaii), 41 years, two months*

John C. Stennis (Democrat-Mississippi), 41 years, two months

Richard B. Russell (Democrat-Georgia), 38 years

Russell B. Long (Democrat-Louisiana), 38 years

Ernest F. Hollings (Democrat-South Carolina), 37 years, three months*

Francis E. Warren (Republican-Wyoming), 37 years

The late **Mike Mansfield** was elected to Congress in 1942 and left it in 1977, which makes him the longest serving senate majority leader in history.

* Currently serving in the Senate

POLITICAL ANAGRAMS

Of what institution is this an anagram?
LOONIES FAR UP THE THAMES
Answer on page 153.

SHAKESPEARE ON POLITICS

Today's spin doctors would have been baffled by Coriolanus's contempt for Rome's citizens. Instead of courting their support, he despised those who would champion him.

CORIOLANUS:
For the mutable rank-scented meiny,
Let them regard me, as I do not flatter,
And therein behold themselves. I say again,
In soothing them we nourish 'gainst our Senate
The cockle of rebellion, insolence, sedition,
Which we ourselves have ploughed for, sowed, and scattered
By mingling them with us, the honoured number
Who lack not virtue, no, nor power, but that
Which they have given to beggars.
Coriolanus, Act III scene i

Width, in centimetres, of Turner's 'The Burning of the Houses of Lords 123 and Commons'. The height is 92 centimetres

Cabinet Ministers don't often resign, but when they do, it usually causes the Government acute embarrassment. Resignations tend to result from a disagreement between the minister and the Prime Minister, or because of a personal scandal. Margaret Thatcher's government had to suffer the resignations of Michael Heseltine (9 January 1986 – the Defence Secretary stormed out of a meeting at No 10 saying, 'If the basis of trust between the Prime Minister and her Defence Secretary no longer exists, there is no place for me with honour in such a Cabinet') and Geoffrey Howe (1 November 1990), while John Major's government became linked with sleaze, thanks in part to David Mellor (24 September, 1992), who resigned after the tabloids gleefully exposed his extra-marital affair.

Some MPs make repeated threats to resign before actually doing so, but it can take the sting out of their decision. The eventual resignation in 2003 of former Labour Secretary of State for International Development, Clare Short, came as something of a damp squib after she retracted an earlier, and very public, threat to leave her post.

The sacking of a Cabinet member is also embarrassing for the government as it never shows the government in a good light. But when it does happen, a Cabinet member is rarely sacked outright. Instead, they are usually given the chance to tender their resignation first. This gives them the chance to exit with a little dignity, though perhaps not without bitterness. When Selwyn Lloyd, Chancellor of the Exchequer from 1960 to 1962, resigned, his letter of resignation to Harold Macmillan read: 'You have told me that you would like me to resign and this I most willingly do.'

QUOTE UNQUOTE

Politics are not my concern...They impressed me as a dog's life without a dog's decencies.
Rudyard Kipling, author

POLITICS IN WRITING

The Queen is most anxious to enlist every one who can speak or write to join in checking this mad, wicked folly of 'Woman's Rights', with all its attendant horrors, on which her poor feeble sex is bent, forgetting every sense of womanly feeling and propriety.
Queen Victoria, letter to Theodore Martin, 29 May 1870

27 BC   **Augustus** – born Octavian in 63 BC, died 14 AD. The first emperor defeated Mark Antony at the battle of Actium in 31 BC.

14 AD   **Tiberius I** – born on 16 November, 42 BC, died 16 March, 37 AD. Adopted by Augustus in 4 AD. Hard and secretive and embittered by neglect.

37 AD   **Caligula** (Gaius Caesar) – born 12 AD, died 41 AD – generally thought to have been insane. Assassinated in a secluded palace corridor by the praetorian tribune Cassius Chaerea and other guardsmen – he was 28.

41 AD   **Claudius I** – born 10 BC, died 54 AD. Began the full-scale annexation of Britain as a Roman province. Thought to have been found hiding behind a curtain and – against his will – declared emperor on the spot by guardsmen after Caligula's assassination. Believed to have been poisoned on the instructions of his fourth wife Aggripina.

54 AD   **Nero** – born Lucius Domitius Ahenobarbus, the son of Aggripina, wife of Claudius. Adopted by Claudius and changed his name to Nero Claudius Caesar. Suspected of setting the fires that destroyed Rome.

68 AD   **Galba** – born 3 BC in Tarracina. Victim of a conspiracy among the praetorians organised by Otho, the governor of Lusitania, and publicly killed. Otho was declared emperor.

69 AD   **Otho** – born at Ferentium in 32 AD. Extravagant and wild as a youth. Had an affair with Nero's mistress Poppaea Sabina, the greatest beauty of her day. Emperor for eight and a half weeks. Committed suicide two weeks before his 37th birthday rather than take on the military leader Aulus Vitellius and plunge Rome into civil war.

69 AD   **Vitellius** – after beating forces loyal to Otho at the First Battle of Bedriacum, Vitellius lost the second to Primus and was killed in hiding.

69 AD   **Vespasian** – born in 9 AD, died in 79 AD. Restored order to a city and government that had been ravaged by civil war. Died peacefully after a short illness.

79-81 AD   **Titus** – born 39 AD. He was educated with Claudius' son Britannicus. Served as a military tribune in Germany and Britain. An affair with the Jewish princess Berenice, 10 years his senior, threatened his succession. His reign was blighted by the eruption of Mount Vesuvius and an outbreak of the plague. He died in 81 AD – possibly poisoned by his brother Domitian with a fish.

Why politicians shouldn't drink:
'OK, so after I surrendered sovereignty... what happened then?'

EXCUSE ME, PRIME MINISTER...

When the BBC's World Affairs Editor, John Simpson, was starting out on BBC radio news in May 1970, he had an unexpected run-in with the Labour Prime Minister, Harold Wilson. He recalls in his book *Strange Places, Questionable People* how on his first assignment for the BBC he was sent out to cover Wilson's departure from London's Euston station, as Wilson was expected to call a snap election.

Surprised by the silence of other reporters when the Prime Minister came into view, the intrepid Simpson showed the sort of chutzpah that would win him fame in later life. He stepped out into the path of Wilson's entourage and thrust his microphone at the Prime Minister. Wilson grabbed the microphone with his left hand and punched Simpson hard in the stomach with his right. As the surprised reporter doubled up, Wilson and his press secretary, Gerald Kaufman, climbed on board their waiting train without looking back. Simpson thought that his career was probably finished. But to his surprise no photographs or accounts of the incident were published, and no complaint was made to the BBC. As Simpson recalled: 'It was a different world... Senior politicians could, it seemed, still get away with – if not murder – then certainly assault and battery.'

Gilbert and Sullivan's opera Iolanthe deals playfully and somewhat irreverently with the subject of politics. In this extract, Strephon, an Arcadian shepherd, is planning to marry his sweetheart Phyllis against the wishes of her ward, the Lord Chancellor. But there's a catch – he is half-man and half-fairy...

Strephon: My brain is a fairy brain, but from the waist downwards I'm a gibbering idiot. My upper half is immortal, but my lower half grows older every day, and some day or other must die of old age. What's to become of my upper half when I've buried my lower half I really don't know!

Fairies: Poor fellow!

Queen: I see your difficulty, but with a fairy brain you should seek an intellectual sphere of action. Let me see. I've a borough or two at my disposal. Would you like to go into Parliament?

Iolanthe: A fairy Member! That would be delightful!

Strephon: I'm afraid I should do no good there – you see, down to the waist, I'm a Tory of the most determined description, but my legs are a couple of confounded Radicals, and, on a division, they'd be sure to take me into the wrong lobby. You see, they're two to one, which is a strong working majority.

Queen: Don't let that distress you; you shall be returned as a Liberal-Conservative, and your legs shall be our peculiar care.

Strephon: (bowing). I see your Majesty does not do things by halves.

Queen: No, we are fairies down to the feet.

RULES OF THE HOUSE

In the absence of a written constitution, parliamentary procedure relies on custom and precedent (as well as a lot of shouting and cheering). Much of this is recorded in certain works of authority, including one in particular, which is *Parliamentary Practice*, written in 1844 by Sir Thomas Erskine May (1815–1886). The Speaker of the House still refers to Erskine May's treatise if there is some dispute about House procedure and no clear rule as to what should be done. *Parliamentary Practice* has been updated regularly by successive Clerks of the House to ensure that solutions to problems are always recorded for future reference.

Erskine May worked in the House of Commons for 55 years, having started as an assistant librarian, and was Clerk of the House from 1871 to 1886. The full title of his book is *A Practical Treatise on the Law, Privileges, Proceedings, and Usage of Parliament*, so it's no surprise that it is mostly referred to simply as 'Erskine May'.

The Spartans' political system was, like their army, a well-oiled machine. Little is known about about the Spartans because, unlike the Athenians, they were not great writers. But fortunately Aristotle, Thucydides and Herodotus had something to say on Sparta.

The Spartans had two kings, who descended from the Agiad and Eurypontid lines and whose duties were largely religious, judicial and military. But apart from the dual kingship, the Spartan ruling class was based on equality. The Spartans referred to each other as homoioi, or 'Similars'. Power and decision-making were shared out in an elaborate checks-and-balances system between the kings, ephors, elders and the assembly. It was an oligarchy – the rule of the few.

Public affairs were first discussed in the Gerousia or Council and then put to the vote in the Assembly, whose members numbered around 3,000. Unusually for ancient Greece, the Council's members held office for life. Women were not allowed to vote.

The five Ephors formed the executive. The Ephorate was elected annually from and by the whole citizen body, and its policies fluctuated with the public mood. The Ephors probably attended the Council regularly and may even have presided over it. Their police powers included rights of arrest over the kings. They were also responsible for foreign affairs. If the Assembly declared war, it was the job of the Ephorate to call up the army.

Spartans dined together at messes or syssitia. Rich or poor, old or young, everyone ate the same food. Spartan men even shared the healthiest wives in the interests of eugenics.

The Spartans didn't extend the principle of equality to the Helots. The equivalent of state serfs, Helots were tied to the lands on which they worked and belonged to the Spartan state. They were not allowed to vote, and were treated brutally. Young Spartans competed in the random slaughter of the slaves on night raids.

The Perioikoi formed an intermediary class between Helot and Spartiate. Resident in neighbouring Messenia and Lakonia, they served under a sort of domestic Spartan empire and were denied the vote.

The Spartans are more famous for their contempt of pleasure and love of honour than for their political system. After eating at a public mess, a Sybarite reportedly exclaimed: 'Now I know why the Spartans do not fear death.' Mothers whose sons died in battle rejoiced. Those whose sons survived defeat were ashamed. According to Plutarch, their parting cry to their sons was, 'Come back with your shield – or on it.'

The best reason for going into politics is to stop people bossing you and me around and to stop them taking away your and my money for no good reason at all.
Boris Johnson, Conservative MP

IT'S A SCANDAL

When one Captain O'Shea filed for a divorce on Christmas Eve 1889, he helped to consign the politician and Irish nationalist hero Charles Stewart Parnell to the political wilderness. Parnell had been having an affair with O'Shea's wife Kitty for some years, and was named in the divorce proceedings. Parnell and Kitty had met in 1880, and Kitty's two children, believed to be Parnell's daughters, were born in 1883 and 1884. In spite of the scandal, Parnell refused to step down from public life. But in December 1890, 44 members of the Irish parliamentary party deserted him and started up their own party with a new leader. Only 27 members had sided with Parnell.

Parnell was no stranger to scandal. *The Times* had published a series of articles in 1887, alleging that the Home Rule leaders had taken part in murder and other crimes during the land war. *The Times* produced letters apparently signed by Parnell, in which he condoned a murder that he had publicly condemned. However, a Special Commission set up to examine the charges cleared the politician. One of the witnesses admitted to forgery and *The Times* had to pay Parnell compensation. Parnell was given a standing ovation in the House of Commons and awarded the freedom of the city of Edinburgh. But it was just at this peak of popularity that O'Shea dropped his bombshell, and Parnell's life was never the same again.

MARCHING FOR PEACE

How far are you prepared to go to make a political point? The followers of Mohandas Karamchand 'Mahatma' Gandhi were prepared to go 241 miles on foot to protest against British India's levy of the salt tax. On 12 March 1930, the Indian revolutionary, who was committed to peaceful protest, set off with 78 followers on a 387.85km march from Sabarmati Ashram in Gujarat. They arrived in the coastal town of Dandi, Gujarat, on 5 April. As part of a sustained campaign of civil disobedience, the 'Salt March' helped keep Indian independence high on the British political agenda.

- First President – James Hanson (not George Washington – Hanson was elected 'President of the United States in Congress Assembled' in 1781, serving one year)
- Shortest President – James Madison, (5ft 4")
- Tallest President – Abraham Lincoln (6ft 4")
- Youngest President – Theodore Roosevelt (42)
- Oldest to take office – Ronald Reagan (69)
- Heaviest President – William Taft (352 lb)
- Presidents who died on Independence Day – John Adams, James Monroe, Thomas Jefferson
- First President born a citizen of the US – Martin Van Buren (born 1782, six years after signing of the Constitution. He was the eighth US President)
- Only President to give all his Federal salary cheques to charity – Herbert Hoover (in government for 47 years)
- First Catholic President – John F Kennedy
- Only President never to marry – James Buchanan
- First to get divorced – Ronald Reagan
- Only Presidents survived by their fathers – John F. Kennedy and Warren Harding
- Only President to be President and not know he was President – David Rice Atchison (President for one Sunday in 1849 after James Knox Polk's term lapsed and before Zachary Taylor could be sworn in)
- Presidents to be arrested: Ulysses S.Grant (speeding on his horse, $20 fine) Franklin Pierce (running over a woman with his horse – case dropped)
- First President to die in office: William Henry Harrison died on 4 April 1841.
- Only President to get a PhD – Woodrow Wilson
- Shortest time in office - William Henry Harrison (one month, 4 March until he caught pneumonia and died on 4 April, 1841)
- Only President not to have been elected to office – Gerald Ford (President Nixon made him his vice president when Spiro Agnew resigned from the post in 1973, and then Ford assumed the presidency when Nixon himself resigned the following year)
- President with shortest middle name – Harry S Truman (the 'S' is not an abbreviation, it is a name; both grandfathers had names beginning with 'S', and it's thought choosing one would offend the other).
- First President to visit China – Richard Nixon
- Only President to get stuck in the bath – William Howard

'I told you before: bigger hat, smaller gun... people are getting the wrong impression!'

PRESIDENTIAL SCANDALS

In December 1998, Bill Clinton became only the second US President in history to be impeached when Congress voted narrowly to impeach him for perjury and obstruction of justice. When Paula Jones decided to sue the President, alleging sexual harassment, she set in motion a scandal that led to Clinton denying he had had sexual relations with a White House intern, Monica Lewinsky. Clinton emphatically denied the story and told the world, 'I want you to listen to me. I'm going to say this again, I did not have sexual relations with that woman, Monica Lewinsky. I never told anybody to lie, not a single time – never. These allegations are false. And I need to go back to work for the American people.' However, Clinton eventually acknowledged the affair in a televised speech to the grand jury on 17 August 1998. In September 1998, Kenneth Starr's four-year investigation into the President was made public in a 445-page report. But Clinton toughed it out and in February 1999 senators voted to acquit him of the impeachment charges.

A pick of the best political websites

www.electoralcommission.org.uk/your-vote/access.cfm Explains the UK electoral register and tells you why voting is a good thing.

www.statelocalgov.net/index.cfm A directory of official state, county and city government websites in the US.

www.lga.gov.uk Everything you ever wanted – and perhaps didn't want – to know about UK local government.

www.direct.gov.uk/Homepage/fs/en Lots of public service information including an A–Z of central and local UK government.

www.parliament.co.uk History and current affairs from the House of Commons and House of Lords.

www.politicalinformation.com Search engine specialising in political information plus links to news media, political history resources and database of international policies

www.csis.org The Center for Strategic and International Studies (CSIS) website offers a vast amount of detailed information on international relations over the last 40 years.

www.politicalresources.net A website containing numerous links to politics-related websites across the globe, sorted by country.

www.realclearpolitics.com Features a daily selection of articles from various US media covering a variety of political standpoints.

www.sosig.ac.uk The Social Science Information Gateway has an extensive Politics section, featuring free resources and book extracts.

www.indymedia.org The Independent Media Centre is a hub for grassroots journalism and has an international database of alternative and amateur reports on various political issues.

www.whitehouse.gov, www.number-10.gov.uk Find a wide range of information about and relating to these residences of power and their inhabitants.

www.mori.com, www.gallup.com, www.nop.co.uk. Stay up to date on the latest polls by checking out the websites of the three biggest opinion research agencies.

www.politicos.co.uk Britain's leading specialist political online bookshop offers an incredible range of books, DVDs, archive material and even memorabilia.

http://europa.eu.int The European Union online. News, functions and MEP contact details in the languages of the EU.

www.nato.int Nato website. News, agenda, opinion and analysis, what is Nato?

www.un.org United Nations website. Member states, main bodies and news in lots of languages.

QUOTE UNQUOTE

Whichever party is in office, the Treasury is in power.
Harold Wilson, Prime Minister 1964–1970, 1974–1976

PRESENTS, PRESENTS, PRESENTS...

Kim Il Sung may be dead, but his memory will live on, as it is written into North Korea's constitution that the 'Great Leader' is his country's 'eternal president'. His son, the living ruler Kim Jong Il, is known as the 'Dear Leader'. Kim Il Sung got his name from a famous Korean guerrilla leader of the early 20th century when he was fighting Japanese occupation forces in the 1930s. He became leader of the Democratic People's Republic of Korea in 1948 and went on to be the world's longest-serving ruler.

North Korea's International Friendship Exhibition Hall, a six-storey temple in the north-western hills near Mt Myohyang, is a shrine to the 'Great Leader'. On Kim's birthday, 15 April, gifts from leaders around the world would pour into the country. There are reportedly 69,378 gifts from 155 countries on display in the hall. Communist leaders Mao Tse-tung and Joseph Stalin sent extravagant green railway cars, Fidel Castro contributed a crocodile-skin briefcase and the Romanian leader Nicolae Ceausescu, apparently a close friend of Kim, marked his friendship with a bear's head mounted on a blood red cushion. The anti-Communist Americans only sent nine presents including a book and two homemade art objects.

Kim also built himself a present, The Tower of the Juche Idea, a 170-metre obelisk with a torch at the top, which rises above the capital Pyongyang. Inside are plaques from 50 study groups in 85 countries dedicated to the Juche ideal, Kim's style of self-reliant communism. Kim had the tower built for his 70th birthday. For his 75th, the 150,000-seat Kim Il Sung stadium was constructed in a vain bid to co-host the 1988 Olympics. The event was given to arch-rivals, South Korea.

POLITICS IN WRITING

Time and the development of our society have rendered the checks and balances, such as they now are, of the constitution of no avail...to restrain an oppressively minded executive if it should win control of a majority of the House of Commons...The path to an 'elected dictatorship' is open and must be blocked now before the bad boys realize their opportunity and organize a takeover of the British Constitution.
Lord Scarman (1911–), *The Shape of Things to Come*

THE LITTLE RED BOOK

The Little Red Book, a title coined in the West, but not used in Russia came to represent the repressive Communist regime in the China of Chairman Mao Tse-tung. The pocket-sized book comprises 33 chapters of Mao's words. There are thought to be over one billion copies in print. Largely because every Chinese person was unofficially required to own, read and carry a copy under Mao. During the upheaval of the Cultural Revolution, those who failed to produce the book on demand could be beaten or given years of hard labour by Mao's Red Guards.

The authorities insisted that the book be read in the workplace as well as in schools. Group sessions were held during office hours. Almost every character depicted on posters and pictures created by the Party's propaganda artists carried a copy of the book. Mao's words were highlighted, and almost all the writing had to quote the leader at some point. But the Revolution wrought economic disaster on China and when it came to an end in 1976, less importance was attached to the book. Mao died on 9 September 1976 and his publicity stunt, so ruthlessly enforced, came to be thought of as a cult of personality.

The Chinese leader declared the People's Republic of China on 1 October 1949. The Communist Party of China still holds power today, but with Mao gone, the Little Red Book no longer commands the terror it once did.

POLITICAL ANAGRAMS

Of what profession is this an anagram?
NO SPECIAL CRITERIA
Answer on page 153.

POLITICS IN WRITING

Latinus himself collapsed under his load of anguish:
The wrath of the gods, the new graves in front of his eyes, told him
Heaven's will was beyond dispute and Aeneas had fate behind him.
Therefore Latinus convened a privy council, commanding
The foremost of his people to appear in his lofty palace.
They came together, their numbers crowding the streets as they flocked
To the royal home. Latinus, the eldest and wielding supreme
Authority, sat in their midst, a gloomy look on his face.

Virgil, *The Aeneid*

THE MASTER'S VOICE

Fidel Castro made the longest speech in the history of the United Nations on 26 September 1960. The Cuban leader went on for four hours and 29 minutes.

PARLIAMENTARY PAY SCALE

	Prime Minister	Cabinet Minister (Commons)	Cabinet Minister (Lords)
1965	14,000	8,500	8,500
1972	20,000	13,000	13,000
1980	34,650	23,500	23,500
1985	41,891	31,271	33,260
1990	46,750	35,120	44,591
1995	57,018	42,834	55,329
1998	102,750	61,650	80,107
1999	107,179	64,307	83,560
2000	110,287	66,172	85,983
2001	113,596	68,157	88,562
2002	116,436	69,861	94,826
2003	119,056	71,433	96,960
2004	121,437	72,862	98,899

THE BILL THAT NEVER WAS

After the Queen gives the Royal Address to open the new session of parliament, the members of the Commons return to their chamber to discuss the issues that have been raised in the speech. However, just to prove a point – the point being that the Commons are not told what to do by anyone, especially not the monarch – they don't go straight to issues raised in the speech, but give first reading to the Outlawries Bill, concerning outlaws and robberies every year. It is not intended to become law.

Sir Thomas Lee summed up the Commons' attitude to the tradition in 1676 when he said he 'cares not how soon the King's Speech is taken into consideration but would not lose the method and order of Parliament. You always begin with reading a Bill'. If this sounds a little petulant, Sir Thomas Meres explained: 'Though forms seem but little things, yet they are of great consequence.'

The practice dates from around 1558 and at first any Bill could be used. Many of them did make progress. But by 1727, when the Outlawries Bill was first debated, the process was just for show. The Outlawries Bill is used every year. It has never been printed and is never introduced by a member (as other Bills are). Its title is, `A Bill for the more effectual preventing clandestine Outlawries.'

Arnold Schwarzenegger's time in front of the camera may have helped the film star win the Californian governorship in October 2003, but what he had been getting up too behind the camera threatened to lose him the election. Schwarzenegger's campaign was hit by accusations of sexual harassment and claims that he had once praised Hitler. Stunt double Rhonda Miller, who worked on two films with the star in the early 1990s, was just one of the women who claimed the body-builder had paid her unwanted sexual attention.

Schwarzenegger denied groping Miller, but on 2 October, the candidate decided to deal with the crisis by making an extraordinary admission: 'So I want to say to you: yes, that I have behaved badly sometimes. Yes, it is true that I was on rowdy movie sets and I have done things that were not right which I thought then was playful, but now I recognize that I have offended people. And to those people that I have offended, I want to say to them: I am deeply sorry about that, and I apologize because this is not what I'm trying to do. When I am governor, I will prove to women that I will be a champion for women. I hope you will give me the chance to prove this.'

The Californian electorate accepted the apology and elected the muscle-man as their governor. It was the first time in the state's history that a governor, Democrat Gray Davis, had been voted out mid-term. Schwarzenegger won just under 50 per cent of the vote. He fought off challenges from a fun-packed list of candidates that included a porn star, the publisher of Hustler magazine and a former child actor.

RULES OF THE HOUSE

Until recently, anyone who was not a member of parliament or an officer of the House – in other words, members of the general public – was known in the House as a 'stranger'.

The public were not always allowed into the debates, and before the House abolished the practice in June 1998, a member could declare 'I spy strangers', which would cause a non-MP to be removed from the public gallery. In the 1870s, an Irish Nationalist Member and Belfast pork merchant called Joseph Biggar caused the Prince of Wales to be removed in this way.

These days MPs can ask 'that this House sit in private'. This happened in December 2001 when the Liberal Democrat Chief Whip Paul Tyler moved that the house sit in private. The motion was agreed to and the House did sit in private but only for a matter of minutes. When the house is sitting in private, no verbatim, sound or television recordings of the session are allowed.

PARLEY WITH ME A WHILE

The word 'Parliament' comes from the French word 'parler' meaning to speak, and the Latin word 'parliamentum', a name for the after-dinner conversations held by monks in their cloisters.

CLOSE CALL

Margaret Thatcher's bathroom was blown apart only minutes after she had left it when the IRA detonated a huge bomb in Brighton's Grand Hotel on 12 October, 1984. The hotel was full of politicians, in town for the Conservative Party Conference. MP Anthony Berry was one of five people to die in the attack. The bomb tore open the front of the hotel on the top floors and masonry fell on guests sleeping below. But although the central section of eight floors crashed into the basement, the Victorian hotel remained standing.

In claiming responsibility for the 'Brighton Hotel Bombing', the IRA announced their intention to try again. 'Today we were unlucky, but remember we only have to be lucky once. You will have to be lucky always.' It was assumed that Thatcher would abandon the conference, but she insisted on continuing, and was back early the next morning to give her address to a hall full of stunned MPs. She responded to the IRA's words with equal defiance: 'This attack has failed. All attempts to destroy democracy by terrorism will fail.'

In September 1986, Patrick Magee was found guilty of the bombing. He was given eight life sentences (including one for a separate offence). He was released from prison in 1999 under the terms of the Good Friday Agreement.

QUOTE UNQUOTE

A politician is an animal who can sit on a fence and yet keep both ears to the ground.
Anon

HER MAJESTY'S STATIONERY OFFICE

Despite the title of this august office, it is not what it seems, as the Queen buys her pencils and rubbers elsewhere. Instead, this government agency, a unit of the Cabinet Office, is a primary source of information for the public, and provides various services. It also controls and administers Crown copyright and administers parliamentary copyright.

Martin Luther King not only helped to break down segregation politics in the United States, but also broke a few records. On 28 August 1963, King led more than 250,000 demonstrators on the largest racial equality rally of all time, to demand civil rights for all. They marched down the Mall in Washington DC before gathering by the Lincoln Memorial to hear King's famous 'Let Freedom Ring' address. 'I have a dream,' he said. 'I have a dream that my four little children will one day live in a nation where they will not be judged by the colour of their skin but by their character.'

A Baptist minister born in Atlanta, Georgia, King became the champion of the civil rights movement in America, although he didn't only fight racism – he also protested against US involvement in Vietnam and against poverty. He was assassinated on 4 April 1968 by James Earl Ray, who pleaded guilty to the murder and was sentenced to 99 years in Tennessee State Penitentiary. A jury of 12 Memphis citizens concluded in 1999 that James Earl Ray was not a lone assassin.

Martin Luther King was the youngest man to be awarded the Nobel Peace Prize, which he received at the age of 35 in 1964. He donated the prize money of $54,123 to the struggle for civil rights.

PRESIDENTIAL SCANDALS

The twenty-ninth President, Warren G Harding, liked a good time. When he ran for president, one of his mistresses, Carrie Phillips, accepted $20,000 from the republican National Committee (the GOP) to keep quiet about their time together. Another mistress, Nan Britton, gave birth to Harding's child in 1919 while he was a senator. As President, Harding continued to 'entertain' Britton, sometimes in a small anteroom off the Oval Office. Britton revealed all in her bestseller, *The President's Daughter*, after Harding's death. Harding had courted controversy from an early age. He married Florence Kling De Wolfe, a divorcee, in 1891 despite the protests of her father Amos Kling. They had no children together.

Harding never publicly spoke of the affair. In 1923 he cryptically asked his Secretary of Commerce, Herbert Hoover 'If you knew of a great scandal in our administration, would you for the good of the country and the party expose it publicly or would you bury it?' Later that year in August Harding died in San Francisco of a heart attack.

PERSONAL CONDUCT

The Committee on Standards in Public Life makes clear the high standards it expects from Members of Parliament...

Selflessness
Holders of public office should take decisions solely in terms of the public interest. They should not do so in order to gain financial or other material benefits for themselves, their family, or their friends.

Integrity
Holders of public office should not place themselves under any financial or other obligation to outside individuals or organisations that might influence them in the performance of their official duties.

Objectivity
In carrying out public business, including make public appointments, awarding contracts, or recommending individuals for rewards and benefits, holders of public office Should make choices on merit.

Accountability
Holders of public office are accountable for their decisions and actions to the public and must submit themselves to whatever scrutiny is appropriate to their office.

Openness
Holders of public office should be as open as possible about all The decisions and actions that they take. They should give reasons for their decisions and restrict information only when the wider public interest clearly demands.

Honesty
Holders of public office have a duty to declare any private interests relating to their public duties and to take steps to resolve any conflicts arising in a way that protects the public interest.

Leadership
Holders of public office should promote and support these principles by leadership and example.

PARTY FUNDS

Critics often claim that the American system is open to money-wielding lobbyists intent on influencing policy, and the figures would seem to bear them out. Federal candidates and national parties raised a combined total of $2.5 billion in funding for their campaigns in 2000. George Bush Senior and Michael Dukakis together spent $92.2 million in 1988. It wasn't cheap in Abraham Lincoln's day either. Lincoln spent $100,000 on his campaign in 1860.

At Westminster, through everything, the Mother of Parliaments remained, a prime target, easily distinguishable, beside the river. The House of Commons Chamber was destroyed: a bomb fell the same night (10 May 1941) through the roof of the Lords, not far from their Chamber. The Palace of Westminster and precincts were hit by ten high explosive bombs, one oil bomb, and many hundreds of incendiaries. St. Thomas's Hospital, across the river, was hit many rimes. Almost every building in sight beside the river was wounded. One morning I left Westminster Pier and saw large holes in the eastern face of Big Ben. But the Speaker was still in his fine house by the Bridge. For the most part, true, they sat during the hours of daylight only: but the doodle-bugs were not afraid of daylight.

It was a pretty grim place to work in, too, during the war. The 'black-out', in such a building, was an almost impossible problem. A few hurricane-lamps on the floor were the only lighting of the great Central Hall, and they made it a lofty tomb of gloom. All the windows went in the early blitzes: the east side was all cardboard and sandbags, and you could not see the river from the Smoking Room. On the terrace was a Guards machine-gun post (of which I went in fear many nights on patrol, in the early days, when E-boats were expected in the Strand). Our favourite pictures and tapestries were taken away, and left depressing gaps. The Harcourt Room was full of beds for the A.R.P.: the lower corridors were anti-gas refuges. The Smoking Room closed earlier - very rightly - to let the staff get home before the blitz. And all the time there was the feeling that the things that mattered were happening elsewhere - a strange sad feeling for the proud M.P. and law-giver. It was pleasant enough for me, after a long voyage up the river from Canvey Island, to pop into the Smoking Room in the evening, hear the gossip and have a drink (if there was any one left), to dart in now and then, with special leave from the Navy, and make a speech about this or that. But I could not have endured to be there all the time: and I honoured those who were.

Alan P Herbert,
Independent Member

TOEING THE PARTY LINE

The expression 'toeing the party line' originated in the Palace of Westminster. During a debate in the House of Commons, MPs must stay behind the two red lines that are marked on the floor of the chamber. When the lines were first drawn, they were placed two swords' lengths plus one foot apart, to ensure that any heated debate did not have unfortunate consequences.

TO KILL A KING

The Thai ruler King Taksin met an unusual end when he allegedly went insane and thought he was Buddha. He was executed using the traditional method of killing a Thai king, which involved putting him into a velvet bag and beating him to death with sandalwood clubs, so that no drop of his blood would touch the ground.

SHORT BUT EFFECTIVE

The former Zambian leader Frederick Chiluba may have won his 1991 election by a large margin, but it was not due to his physical stature. The five foot (1.52m) tall President of Zambia was a trades union official before he swept to election victory with a landslide in 1991. The diminutive Chiluba won a further five year term in 1996. He divorced his wife Vera, with whom he has nine children, in 2001 and was replaced as president in January 2002 at the end of his term by his one-time Vice President, Levy Mwanawasa.

QUOTE UNQUOTE

There are three classes which need sanctuary more than others – birds, wild flowers and Prime Ministers.
Stanley Baldwin, Prime Minister 1923–1924, 1924–1929, 1935–1937

EGG ON THEIR FACES

Enoch Powell – pelted with eggs during the 1970 general election campaign in Eltham, South East London. Powell was supporting the Conservative candidate John Jackson.

John Prescott – an egg was thrown at the Deputy Prime Minister in Wales during the 2001 General Election. Prescott responded by landing his famous punch on the protester.

Arnold Schwarzenegger – hit on his left shoulder by an egg during his 2003 campaign to become the governor of California, the fifth largest economy in the world. Schwarzenegger continued with his address while an aide tried to tidy him up.

Bill Clinton – after the former president was struck by an egg on a speaking tour of Warsaw in May 2001, an aide said, 'It is good for young people to be angry about something.'

Norman Tebbit once said: 'Those who scream and throw eggs are not the real unemployed. If they were really hard up, they would be eating them.

HOW TO MAKE A CABINET

Important moments in the history of the British Cabinet

1949 Churchill experiments with a Cabinet of 16 'overlords' during World War Two and continued using them afterwards so as not to have to deal with such large numbers of ministers.

1962 Macmillan abruptly sacks six members of his cabinet because of the government's general unpopularity. Became known as the 'night of the long knives'.

1964 Ministers are granted their own special advisers and Wilson creates a Political Office at No 10.

1970 The super-ministries of the Department of Trade and Industry and the Department of the Environment are created.

1975 When the Cabinet was split over the referendum on the UK joining the EC, Harold Wilson suspended Collective Responsibility to allow Cabinet members to campaign on opposite sides, an unprecedented move.

1977 Collective responsibility again suspended over the issue of which voting system should be used in EC elections.

1983 Cabinet Secretary becomes head of the civil service.

1989 The Chancellor of the Exchequer, Nigel Lawson, resigns from government, criticising Thatcher's leadership and her use of economic advisers.

1990 The Deputy Prime Minister Sir Geoffrey Howe resigns from the Cabinet, also criticising Thatcher's leadership.

1990 John Major introduces a more collegiate style of Cabinet government.

1994 Ignoring the principle of cabinet responsibility, Michael Portillo criticises the government's EU policy.

1996 Cabinet Secretary Sir Robin Butler objects to government plans to use the Civil Service to promote its policies.

POLITICAL ANAGRAMS

Of which government is this an anagram?
DUH? ... I AIN'T BIN SO SMART
Answer on page 153.

'I feel ridiculous too, Gordon, but I can't risk being jeered at by the WI two years in a row...'

IT'S A SCANDAL

When the Royal British Bank crashed in 1857, it took with it the political career of John McGregor, a Liberal MP for Glasgow. Elected to Parliament in 1847, McGregor was chairman of the bank from which 'he helped himself' to the not insignificant sum of £8,000. When the bank collapsed, his pilfering was revealed. He resigned his seat in Parliament but died before his case came to trial. However, his colleague on the bank's board, Humphrey Brown, Liberal member for Tewkesbury, did not escape prison. He had taken out £30,000 and was in debt to the tune of £77,000. He was charged with conspiracy to defraud and spent six months behind bars. However, he later twice stood for election in Tewkesbury – both times unsuccessfully. Despite his chutzpah, the votors were not impressed; in the by-election of 1859, he failed to win a single vote.

On 11 September 2001, on a sunny morning in New York, the unimaginable became possible when at 08.48 American Airlines Flight 11 crashed into the north tower of the World Trade Centre. As the world's cameras trained on its burning twin, the second tower was hit by a second plane at 09.03. As the shockwaves spread around the world, it was clear that this was no accident.

President George W Bush was in Florida reading to schoolchildren when he was informed of the attack. At 09.40 American Airlines Flight 77 struck the Pentagon, the nerve centre of the US military. Of the 194 people who died in this crash, 125 were in the Pentagon building and 64 were passengers and crew on the plane. The remaining five were hijackers. President Bush authorised the shooting down of any plane that threatened Washington. The White House and The Capitol were evacuated.

A passenger flying to San Francisco got through to an emergency despatcher on his mobile phone at 09.58, saying: 'We are being hijacked, we are being hijacked.' United Airlines Flight 93 slammed into the ground 80 miles south east of Pittsburgh at 10.03. Forty-one people lost their lives as well as the four hijackers. There were no survivors. Transcripts of the passengers' mobile phone conversations suggested that they attempted to overpower the hijackers, once they heard about the fate of the Twin Towers.

In New York, the horror was unfolding. The south tower collapsed at 10.05, shrouding the Manhattan skyline in smoke. Emergency workers and firefighters were crushed as they raced to save lives. On a normal day, 50,000 people worked in the Twin Towers.

The north tower imploded at 10.29, showering dust and devastation on the streets below. New York's mayor Rudy Giuliani warned that the unknown death toll might be 'more than any of us can bear'. It was. But far fewer lives were lost than initially feared. More than two years after the attacks, New York reduced its official death toll by 40 people down from 2,792 to 2,752.

'Today,' announced a stunned President Bush, 'our fellow citizens, our freedom, our way of life came under attack.' The sheer scale and the implications of September 11 rocked the world order. The financial and military might of the only remaining superpower had been shown to be defenceless in the face of a terrorist onslaught, which had been carried out by a mere 11 hijackers. The suicide bomber had become an international force.

DAMNED LIES?

According to polls in 2004, the following is true...

74% of Britons feel they have a duty to vote in a general election, although only **51%** said they definitely would vote.

59% of people cannot name their own MP.

38% of Britons have discussed politics or the political news in the past three years.

32% were satisfied with the way their MP does his or her job.

27% of people said they trust politicians.

FALSE PROMISES

Politicians in Malaysia were criticised during a recent general election for promising voters a place in Heaven. The government complained that some Islamic parties used the bribe as an unfair tactic. The Electoral Commission also took a dim view. It said that luring voters with the promise of a blessed afterlife was 'illogical and could be disadvantageous to the other candidates.' It added: 'How do you justify saying that anyone who votes for you will go to Heaven?'

POLITICS IN WRITING

Early the following year Mosley visited Mussolini's Italy. He concluded that parliamentary politics had had its day and that the dictatorships springing up around Europe were the way forward. On his return therefore he started planning a fascist movement, British-style, which bore fruit in October 1932 as the British Union of Fascists (BUF). Initially influenced by Italian fascism, the BUF in its early couple of years was relatively successful and great efforts were expended to gain respectability amongst the traditional right, which was achieved amongst some Conservatives.

But this was all undermined by the violence that was clearly on how at the party's June 1934 rally at Olympia. The true face of ug.y extremism and anti-Semitism was made plain for all to see, and from later that year anti-Semitism became a major policy theme of the BUF. These events lost the party any middle-class support it might have hoped to get (and quite a lot of its membership), and it took its arguments (and violence) to the streets.

The Politico's Book of the Dead, **edited by Iain Dale**

John Profumo was the Secretary of State for War in the Conservative Macmillan government in the sixties. Profumo was married to actress Valerie Hobson but he had a brief affair with a Soho show girl, Christine Keeler. The pair met when a party arranged by Profumo's close friend Lord Astor joined forces with another gathering organised by the London doctor Stephen Ward on the Cliveden Estate in Buckinghamshire in 1961. Keeler and Profumo went on their first 'date' in the ministerial limousine. Sir Norman Brook, the Cabinet Secretary, warned the minister about the dangers of the affair. Profumo ended the relationship after a matter of weeks.

In 1962 the affair became public and it emerged that Keeler was also involved with an attaché at the Russian Embassy called Yevgeny 'Eugene' Ivanov. The Russian had been at the party where Profumo first met Keeler. They had fought for the call-girl's attention in the pool. Profumo denied that there was any impropriety in his relationship with Keeler in March 1963 but in June he admitted to misleading the House and resigned.

Lord Denning produced an official report into the affair on 25 September which criticised the government's handling of events, but did not suggest any breach of security. The Tory Prime Minister Harold Macmillan resigned due to ill health soon afterwards. Meanwhile Ward was prosecuted for living off immoral earnings and committed suicide in August. Keeler escaped any penalty for her part in the affair, although she was sentenced to nine months in prison for an unrelated perjury charge. She later claimed in her autobiography that Ward was a Soviet spy and had asked her to procure secret documents from Profumo, and that the exposure of her affair with Profumo was to cover up a breach in government security.

POLITICS IN WRITING

Consider, for instance, the ridiculousness of the division of parties into 'Liberal' and 'Conservative'. There is no opposition whatever between those two kinds of men. There is opposition between the Liberals and Illiberals; that is to say, between people who desire liberty, and who dislike it. I am a violent Illiberal; but it does not follow that I must be a Conservative. A Conservative is a person who wishes to keep things as they are; and he is opposed to a Destructive, who wishes to destroy them, or to an Innovator, who wishes to alter them. Now, though I am an Illiberal, there are many things I should like to destroy.

John Ruskin, *Fors Clavigera*

PARLIAMENTARY GLOSSARY

Abstention – an MP's refusal to vote on a motion

Adjournment of the House – the request by a Commons MP to end proceedings for the day

Admonition – the rebuke of a misbehaving MP by the Speaker of the House of Commons

Bar of the House – the line marked by a leather strip at the entrance to the Commons which only MPs may cross

Bill – the draft of an Act of Parliament which is presented to either House for a vote. It becomes an Act when Royal Assent is granted.

Black Rod – the officer of the Royal Household who supervises the doorkeepers and messengers of the House of Lords. It is also Black Rod who issues the orders for entry into the Stranger's Gallery.

Catching the Speaker's eye – MPs in the Commons who want to speak must stand and await permission from the speaker.

Count – the Speaker can close the House if there are fewer than 40 MPs present

Crossing the floor – MPs who switch party allegiance signal their intent by crossing the floor of the House.

Dissolution – when the king or queen terminates the Parliament of the House of Commons. A general election ensues.

Father of the House – The longest serving MP in the House of Commons.

Front benches – where Government members and senior opposition members sit

Government bill – a bill which is introduced by a government minister

Hansard – the written reports of House of Commons business

Maiden speech – an MP's first Commons speech. The Speaker traditionally gives preference to an MP making his first speech.

Minority Government – a government formed by a party without a majority of seats. To remain in government it must retain the confidence of the House of Commons.

Oath of allegiance – the oath of loyalty to the Sovereign that each MP must take before taking a seat in the Commons.

Order paper – timetable of daily events in either House.

Parliamentary procedure – the rules according to which the House of Commons and house of Lords conduct business.

Point of order – an MP can bring to the attention of the Speaker a technical or procedural breach of order at any time during a debate or other House business. The Speaker's decision on the validity of the point is final.

Question time – when members of the two Houses put questions to ministers.

Recess – time between two Parliaments

Teller – the counter of ayes and noes appointed by the Speaker.

Ten-minute rule – MPs have ten minutes to make their comments or statements.

CARTOON CAPERS

The official symbol of the Republican Party is an elephant thanks to Thomas Nast (1840–1902), a caricaturist and editorial cartoonist in the 19th century. In the 1870s, the question of President Ulysses S Grant running for office for a third consecutive term was raised by the *New York Herald* (as 'Caesarism'), and was worrying the Democrats. Nast took this idea and brought it to life by mixing it with another story of the day which had run in the *New York Herald*, this one totally untrue. It reported that animals had escaped from a zoo and were hunting prey in Central Park. In an edition of *Harper's Weekly* Nast drew a picture of a jackass (representing the Herald) in a lion's skin (the threat of Caesarism) frightening off animals in the forest (Central Park), one of which was an elephant (the Republican vote). When the Republicans fared badly in the 1874 election Nast drew another cartoon depicting an elephant in a trap to illustrate how voters normally allied to the Republican Party were tricked. The Republicans soon adopted the elephant as their symbol, and the Democrats, showing an admirable sense of humour, duly accepted the donkey as theirs.

IT'S A SCANDAL

James O'Shea's biography *Prince of Swindlers* has helped to shed light on the scandalous life of the MP John Sadleir. Elected as a Liberal, Sadleir joined a group of nationalist-minded MPs known as the Irish Brigade or the Pope's Brass Band. Nevertheless, he didn't say no to a government post as Junior Lord of the Treasury in Gladstone's new administration of 1852 to the chagrin of his fellow Irish Brigadiers. Sadleir forged deeds as collateral for loans on London banks. His debts jeopardised his banks in London and Dublin. In desperation, he became more reckless in his attempts to rescue the situation.

Thousands were ruined in the crash. On 16 February 1856, he committed suicide. Sadleir had blamed himself for 'numberless crimes of a diabolical character' in letters to friends just before his death. *The Nation* described Sadleir as 'a sallow-faced man with multifarious intrigue, cold, callous, cunning'. There was a rumour that he wasn't dead at all but had escaped to America.

Sadleir's brother James, also an MP, had tried to discourage his brother from his fraudulent behaviour, but ended up stealing money himself to protect John, and himself had to flee abroad after his brother's death. He settled in Zurich, but was murdered in 1881 while out walking.

Just a smidgeon of the scandal and subterfuge to rock the government in recent years

Jonathan Aitken and the arms to Nigeria, *1971*

Future Tory MP Jonathan Aitken gave the *Sunday Telegraph* a copy of a document, the Scott report, which seemed to show that Britain was supplying far more arms to Nigeria than the government acknowledged. He had been shown the report by General Henry Alexander, a British representative with the International Military Observer team in Nigeria. Aitken was charged with breaking the Official Secrets Act but was cleared at the Old Bailey.

Sarah Tisdall and Cruise missiles, *1984*

A Foreign Office clerk called Sarah Tisdall, was sentenced to six months in prison after she released information to *The Guardian*. Tisdall believed that Michael Heseltine, was misleading the public about the arrival of Cruise missiles at Greenham Common in order to reduce public opposition.

Political vetting in the BBC

It emerged in 1985 that the BBC had used MI5 to vet a job applicant. The BBC was forced to bring the practice to an end.

Spycatcher, *1987–1988*

Margaret Thatcher's government tried to ban a book written by Peter Wright, a retired MI5 agent living in Tasmania. Wright alleged among other things that there had been an MI5 conspiracy to destabilise Harold Wilson's government between 1974 and 1976. The government dispatched the Cabinet secretary, Sir Robert Armstrong, to Australia in an attempt to ban the book there, but during the trial, Armstrong admitted that the government had been 'economical with the truth'. The case was dismissed.

Spying on the EU, *1991*

A *Guardian*/ITN World in Action investigation presented evidence from Robin Robison, an ex-security services official, that the security services regularly engage in unauthorised spying on Britain's EU partners to find out their negotiating positions.

Surveillance of MPs and ministers

The memoirs of Alan Clark suggested that MPs and ministers are under MI5 surveillance. He was not the first; MPs Jonathan Aitken and Sir Richard Body had already made the same claim.

Clare Short, *2004*

Former Secretary of State for International Development Clare Short claimed that British spies listened in to UN Secretary General Kofi Annan's office in the run up to the Iraq war. Tony Blair, described the claims as 'deeply irresponsible'.

POLITICAL ANAGRAMS

Of which foreign leader is this an anagram?
OH, RAN ISRAEL
Answer on page 153.

THE LOONY ELEMENT

There are those who take electioneering seriously and those who don't. Born in 1940, David Edward Sutch changed his name by deed poll in the 1960s to Screaming Lord Sutch, 3rd Earl of Harrow, and set up the Monster Raving Loony Party in 1963. In 1983, he became the longest-serving leader of any political party.

Lord Sutch fought and lost more elections than any other British politician. He increased his chances by standing in by-elections as well as General Elections. In all, he compiled 15,657 votes. His most successful campaign was the 1994 by-election in Rotherham when he won 1,114 votes.

Lord Sutch was found hanged at his home in June 1999. A memorial to him has been erected in the small mid-Wales town of Llanwrtyd Wells. The top hat and rosette sculpture marks the starting point for an annual race contested by horses and humans, in which, true to form, Lord Sutch was a regular competitor.

The maverick may be dead, but his party lives on. Alan Howling Lord Hope replaced Sutch as the leader of the Official Monster Raving Loony Party. Policies include working together with Volkswagen to produce a new car that runs on farmyard effluent. The aim is to prevent a fuel crisis and to help farmers.

I WAS JUST LEAVING

MPs who have swapped sides

David Owen and Bill Rodgers were Labour MPs when they left to join the Social Democratic Party in 1981.

Emma Nicholson defected from Conservative to LibDems in 1995.

Reg Prentice, a Cabinet Minister, defected from the Labour government of 1974–1979 to join the Conservatives.

John Horam represented Labour, Conservative and the SDP during his political career.

Peter Thurnham defected from Conservative to Liberal Democrats in 1996.

George Gardiner, Conservative MP for Reigate, defected to the Referendum Party in 1997.

Shaun Woodward was Conservative MP for Witney until, after being sacked from the front bench, he defected to Labour in 1999.

DURING THE COMPILATION OF THIS BOOK, THE COMPANION TEAM...

Had breakfast in 37 different constituencies

Experimented with proportional representation and accidentally elected a stapler as their leader

Met 43 male politicians from 11 different parties, of whom only three wore cufflinks

Snagged themselves five times on a hanging chad

Found 11 different spellings of Gaddafi, and invented two more

Actually met a man called Olly Garky

Discovered that a week is an even longer time in book compilation

Read 17 manifestos and counted the word 'pledge' 349 times.

Realised that there were the exact same number of living ex US presidents as living ex British prime ministers

Debated frequently the respective merits of Bakuninian and Kropotkinian anarchism

Remarked that things aren't what they used to be

Formed their own political party, stormed to power, strayed from their principles, but returned in a blaze of egalitarian economic glory once they'd abandoned the stapler

Please note that although every effort has been made to ensure accuracy in this book, the above statistics may be the result of spinning minds.

There seem to me very few facts,
at least ascertainable facts, in politics

Sir Robert Peel, Prime Minister,
1834–1835 and 1841–1846

The answers. As if you needed them.

P14.   50%

P24.   Heath (Edward)

P29.   Ike (Eisenhower)

P39.   Kinshasa

P47.   Mandela (Nelson)

P52.   Clinton (Bill)

P59.   BLAIR – FLAIR – FLAIL – FRAIL – TRAIL – TRAIN – BRAIN – BRAWN – BROWN

P71.   Baroness Thatcher, The Iron Lady

P81.   Tony Blair MP

P89.   William Ewart Gladstone

P97.   Sir Anthony Hammond
       Sir Anthony was given the task of investigating the conduct of Peter Mandelson in the Hinduja passport affair (early 2001) but found him to be completely blameless.

P101. Lord Brian Hutton
       The inquiry into the death of Dr David Kelly concluded this year. The report cleared Blair of all responsibility.

P108. Re-constructing Iraq

P115. Weapons of Mass Destruction

P123. The Houses of Parliament

P134. Career politicians

P142. Bush Administration

P151. Ariel Sharon

IDEOLOGIES, POLITICAL PHILOSOPHIES AND PLANS FOR OFFICE

FURTHER READING

Essential Central Government 2002, Ron Fenney

Essential Local Government 2002, Ron Fenney

The Hutchinson Almanac 2000

2201 Fascinating Facts, David Louis

The Political Animal, Jeremy Paxman

The Oxford Dictionary of Political Quotations, Antony Jay

The New Century, Eric Hobsbawm

The Ultimate Book of Lists, edited by Michael Cader

The Proud Highway, Hunter S Thompson

Politics' Strangest Characters, Neil Hamilton

Athens and Sparta, Anton Powell

Formation of the European Empires 1488–1920, Muriel E Chamberlain

Sparta, edited by Michael Whitby

The New British Politics, Ian Budge, Ivor Crewe, David McKay and Ken Newton

The Penguin Dictionary of Political Quotations, compiled by Robert Stewart

Reader's Digest Book of Facts: People, Places, Science & Technology, Animals & Plants, Arts & Entertainment, the Earth, the Universe, Reader's Digest Editors

The Times Atlas of World History

More George W Bushisms, Jacob Weisberg

Modern England, RK Webb

The House Magazine

The Complete Works of William Shakespeare

www.anagramgenius.com and www.anagrammy.com

ACKNOWLEDGEMENTS

We gratefully acknowledge permission to reprint extracts of copyright material in this book from the following authors, publishers and executors:

Extract from *And Now Tomorrow by* Vernon Bartlett. Reproduced by permission of Pollinger Limited and the Proprietor.

Epitaph on the Politician Himself by Hilaire Belloc, copyright © estate of Hilaire Belloc 1970 reproduced by permission of PFD on behalf of The Estate of Hilaire Belloc. Copyright © Estate of Hilaire Belloc 1970.

Extract from *The Man of Destiny* by George Bernard Shaw, reproduced by permission of the Society of Authors on behalf of the Bernard Shaw Estate

Extract from *In Place of Fear* by Aneurin Bevan reproduced by permission of Quartet Books

Extract from *Diaries: Into Power* by Alan Clark, published by Weidenfeld & Nicolson, a division of the Orion Publishing Group.

Extract from *Politico's Book of the Dead*, edited by Iain Dale, copyright © Matthew Seward, reproduced by permission of Methuen Ltd

Extract from *Politics' Strangest Characters* by Neil Hamilton reproduced by permission of Robson Books

Extract from *Independent Member* by Alan Herbert, published by Methuen Books. Reproduced by permission of AP Watt Ltd on behalf of the Estate of Jocelyn Herbert and Teresa Elizabeth Perkins.

Extract from *On the Edge of the New Century* by Eric Hobsbawm, published by Abacus. Reproduced by permission of Gius. Laterza & Figli SpA, Roma-Bari.

Extract from *The Iliad* by Homer, translated by Martin Hammond (Penguin Classics, 1987). Copyright c Martin Hammond 1987.

Extract from *The Odyssey* by Homer, translated by E V Rieu and Dominic Rieu (Penguin Classics 1946, revised edition 1991). Copyright c 1946 by E V Rieu. This revised translation copyright c the Estate of the late E V Rieu, and D C H Rieu, 1991.

Extract from *Churchill* by Roy Jenkins (copyright c Estate of Roy Jenkins 2001) reproduced by permission of PFD (www.pfd.co.uk) on behalf of the Estate of Roy Jenkins and Pan Macmillan

Adams, John Quincy 73
Addington, Henry 95
Alcohol and drugs 81, 100
Ambition 61, 96
Ancient influences 31, 43, 47, 49, 101, 108, 125, 128
Apartheid 86
Assassination attempts 18, 45, 63, 84, 109
Assassinations 10, 23, 24, 40, 79, 121, 138, 141
Attlee, Clement, 43, 92
Baldwin, Stanley
Balfour, Arthur 61
Bartlett, Vernon 116
Belloc, Hilaire 53
Bevan, Aneurin 25, 64
Bierce, Ambrose 34
Birthdays 51
British Prime Ministers 11, 13, 19, 28, 38, 50, 61, 74, 80, 81, 91, 112, 113,122, 126, 137
Boothroyd, Betty 68
Boycotts, demonstrations and petitions 77, 86, 129, 138
Bush, George 80
Bush, George W 62
Callahan, James 38, 58
Castro, Fidel 135
Celes, Dr John 109
Chaplin, Charlie 113
Chinese Leaders 73
Churchill, Winston, 19, 43, 44, 99, 118,
Corruption 46, 85, 106, 114, 121, 143, 143, 148
Curiosities 23
Dale, Iain 145
de Gaulle, Charles 99
Demise of Communism 117, 134
Demises 32, 36, 65, 79, 90
Despots and dictators 10, 47, 120, 133
Disraeli, Benjamin 57, 66

Djilas, Milovan 39
Douglas-Home, Sir Alex 57
Election casualties 16, 18
Election fraud 46, 95, 145
Election records 42, 67, 113, 150
Elections 21, 23, 25, 27, 53, 55, 141,
European Union the 27, 46, 64, 107
Executions 11, 29, 33, 36, 65, 74, 77, 78
Explosive protests 28, 29, 137, 141
Facts and figures 22, 26, 32, 80, 91, 117, 132, 147
Films 66
First families 16, 47, 48, 65, 74
First ladies 23, 25, 28, 49, 68, 69, 71, 93, 114, 115, 124
Fisticuffs 15, 61, 103, 126
Flags and symbols 60, 70, 148
Freemasons 91
Gandhi, Mahatma 129
Gladstone, William 84
Gore, Al 32
Grant, Daphne 89
Health Service, the 64
Herbert, Alan P 140
Hobsbawm, Eric 94
Homer 43, 115
House of Commons 10, 57, 68, 81, 92, 95, 102, 115, 135, 136, 139, 140,
House of Lords 11, 19, 71, 88,
Houses of Parliament 24, 29, 73,
Iron Curtain, the 118
Jefferson, Thomas 34
Jenkins, Roy 19
Johnson, Boris 59,
Johnson, Lyndon B 120
Kennedy, John F 25
Kinnock, Neil 102
Kipling, Rudyard 124
Lamon, Ward Hill 105

Livingstone, Ken 77
Lloyd George, David 74
Lord Chancellor, the 112
Mandela, Nelson 71, 110
Mansfield, Michael 103
Mao, Tsetung 65, 134
May, Erskine 127
Media, the 16, 17, 50, 56, 59, 63, 98, 121, 126, 129
Memoirs 76, 90
Mencken, HL 63
Monarchs 40, 67, 77, 90, 124, 135, 137, 141
Moncrieff, Chris 98
More, Thomas 74
Murder 36, 65
Nato members 75
Nick names 52
Oddities 35, 55, 74, 115
Old timers 22, 26, 33, 43, 94
Origins 25, 47, 58, 70, 97, 137, 140, 147
Paine, Thomas 27
Paxman, Jeremy 16
Peccadilloes 35, 49, 65, 66, 67, 101, 105, 120, 129, 131, 136, 138, 146, 148
Peculiar political parties 100
Peron, Eva 114
Plato 49
Political animals 12, 116, 141, 145
Politician's pied-a-terres 11, 13, 51, 72, 78, 82
Politician's wives 16, 105, 121
Pressure groups 120
Puzzles and anagrams 14, 24, 29, 39, 52, 59, 71, 81, 89, 97, 101, 109, 115
Reagan, Ronald 22
Rentoul, John 11
Reputations (lost) 16, 35, 47, 50, 90, 106, 114
Resignations 30, 38, 42, 50, 67, 124, 142
Revolution 33
Riddell, Peter 56

Right to stand 19, 22, 37
Robinson, Adam 51
Roosevelt, Franklin D 93, 113
Rumsfeld, Donald 68
Ruskin, John 146
Scarman, Lord 133
Sexual politics 23, 33, 64, 100, 120, 124
Shakespeare, William 17, 21, 41, 60, 75, 88
Shaw, G B 78
Simpson, John 126
Slavery 87, 108
Sleaze 16, 143
Snuff in the House 9
Sophocles 99
Speaker, the 54, 65, 68
Speeches 39, 44, 62, 116, 135
Spin 28, 38, 50
Spitting Image 59, 87
Sporting politicians 97, 106, 119
Stevenson, Adlai 15
Tecumseh's curse 79
Thatcher, Margaret 18, 28, 49
Traditions 10, 11, 19, 30, 47, 52, 57, 68, 71, 73, 81, 88, 92, 95, 102, 104, 111, 115, 127, 135, 136, 140
Trollope, Anthony 32
Truman, Harry S 55,
UK dependent territories 35
US Declaration of Independence, the 64
US Presidents 17, 23, 32, 55, 72, 76, 79, 94, 103, 106, 109, 116, 121, 131
Virgil 134
von Bismark, Otto 115
Wars and disputes 14, 20, 28, 64, 144,
Waugh, Evelyn 74
Wellesley, Arthur 116
Whitehorn, Katherine 109
Wilmington, Earl of 48
Wilson, Harold 133
Yeats, WB 38
Ziegler, Philip 67

The Cook's Companion
Whether your taste is for foie gras or fry-ups, this tasty compilation is an essential ingredient in any kitchen, boiling over with foodie facts, fiction, science, history and trivia.
ISBN 1-86105-772-5

The Gardener's Companion
For anyone who has ever put on a pair of gloves, picked up a spade and gone out into the garden in search of flowers, beauty and inspiration.
ISBN 1-86105-771-7

The Literary Companion
Whether your Dickens is Charles or Monica, your Stein Gertrude or Franken, this is the book for you. The full range of literary fact and fiction from Rebecca East to Vita Sackville-West.
ISBN 1-86105-798-9

The London Companion
From Edgware to Morden, Upminster to Ealing, here's your chance to explore the history, mystery and many peculiarities of the most exciting capital city in the world.
ISBN 1-86105-799-7

The Moviegoer's Companion
Explore the strange and wonderful world of movies, actors, cinemas and salty popcorn in all their glamorous glory from film noir to Matt LeBlanc.
ISBN 1-86105-797-0

The Traveller's Companion
For anyone who's ever stared at a distant plane, wondered where it's going, and spent the rest of the day dreaming of faraway lands and ignoring everything and everyone else.
ISBN 1-86105-773-3

The Walker's Companion
If you've ever laced a sturdy boot, packed a cheese and pickle sandwich, and put one foot in front of the other in search of stimulation and contemplation, then this book is for you.
ISBN 1-86105-825-X

The Wildlife Companion
Animal amazements, ornithological oddities and botanical beauties abound in this compilation of natural need-to-knows and nonsense for wildlife-lovers everywhere.
ISBN 1-86105-770-9